The Third Way and
its Critics

Anthony Giddens

The Third Way
and its Critics

Polity

First published in 2000 by Polity Press
in association with Blackwell Publishers Ltd.

Reprinted 2001

Editorial office:
Polity Press
65 Bridge Street
Cambridge CB2 1UR, UK

Marketing and production:
Blackwell Publishers Ltd
108 Cowley Road
Oxford OX4 1JF, UK

Published in the USA by
Blackwell Publishers Inc.
Commerce Place
350 Main Street
Malden, MA 02148, USA

ISBN 0-7456-2449-9
ISBN 0-7456-2450-2 (pbk)

A catalogue record for this book is available from the British Library and has been applied for from the Library of Congress.

Typeset in 11 on 14 pt Sabon
by Ace Filmsetting Ltd, Frome, Somerset
Printed in Great Britain by T. J. International, Padstow, Cornwall

This book is printed on acid-free paper.

Contents

Preface

This work is written as a sequel to my book *The Third Way*, first published in the autumn of 1998. The work attracted a great deal of interest and quite a bit of criticism too. In this current volume, I expand upon some of the themes outlined in the earlier study and discuss the criticisms commonly made of the idea of the third way. Not wishing to write a review of reviews, I haven't responded to critiques of my book as such. Instead, I have concentrated upon criticisms made more generally of third way politics.

The Third Way appeared shortly after the high-point of the Asian crisis. In the wake of that crisis the hold of rightist thinking over politics has diminished. Almost everywhere, at least for the moment, conservatism is in retreat. The rise of third way politics is partly a reaction to this situation, but has also to some extent helped bring it about. The energies of many on the political left have long been preoccupied with resisting neoliberal claims, or with a defensive reworking of leftist thought in the face of them. Those energies can now be channelled in a more positive direction. Third way politics, I try to show, isn't an ephemeral set of ideas. It will continue to have its dissenters and critics. But it will be at the core of political dialogues in the years to come, much as neo-liberalism was until recently and old-style social democracy was before that. Third way politics will be the point of view with which others will have to engage.

Acknowledgements

I should like to thank the many people who have helped in the preparation of this book. David Held read and commented on successive drafts of the manuscript. I owe a great deal to him. I also owe a debt of thanks to Will Hutton, with whom I have had numerous political discussions over the past few months. I have learned a lot from our dialogues. Will made valuable comments on an early draft of the book. David Miliband and Sidney Blumenthal provided very useful further observations and reactions. Alena Ledeneva provided support, help and inspiration throughout.

Miriam Clarke worked tirelessly on the manuscript and I am extremely grateful to her for her diligence and good humour in so doing. Boris Holzer worked as my research assistant while I was writing the book and was a great source of help. My thanks are due also to the following: Alison Cheevers, Anne de Sayrah and Amanda Goodall.

A.G.
November 1999

1

The Third Way and its Critics

The idea of finding a third way in politics has become a focus of controversy across the world. The term 'third way', of course, is far from new, having been employed by groups of diverse political persuasions in the past, including some from the extreme right. Social democrats, however, have made use of it most often. During the Cold War period, many saw social democracy itself as a third way, distinct from American market liberalism on the one side and Soviet communism on the other. The term largely dropped out of sight for some while, before being resurrected in political dialogues of the past few years.

Curiously, the current popularity of the concept of the third way comes from its introduction into contexts in which it had never appeared before – the United States and Britain. Its revival, and subsequent wide diffusion, owes much to its adoption in those countries – by the Democrats and the Labour Party. Each party reshaped its political outlook, as well as its more concrete approaches to getting elected. Terminologically they resembled one another: the relabelling of the American party as the New Democrats was rapidly followed by the creation of New Labour in the UK.

The third way was originally described by the American Democrats as a 'new progressivism'. *The New Progressive Declaration*, published by the Democratic Leadership Council in 1996, argued that a fresh beginning in politics was called for to cope with a world in fundamental change.[1] In the first progressive era, in the early part of the twentieth century, American left-of-centre politics was radically reshaped in response to rapid industrialization and urbanism. The New Deal was based on collaboration between the state, the labour unions and big business.

Today, however, the 'big institutions', the New Democrats argued, can no longer deliver on the social contract as they did before. The advent of new global markets, and the knowledge economy, coupled with the ending of the Cold War, have affected the capability of national governments to manage economic life and provide an ever-expanding range of social benefits. We need to introduce a different framework, one that avoids both the bureaucratic, top-down government favoured by the old left and the aspiration of the right to dismantle government altogether.

The cornerstones of the new progressivism are said to be equal opportunity, personal responsibility and the mobilizing of citizens and communities. With rights come responsibilities. We have to find ways of taking care of ourselves,

[1] Democratic Leadership Council–Progressive Policy Institute, *The New Progressive Declaration*. Washington, DC: DLC–PPI, 1996.

because we can't now rely on the big institutions to do so. Public policy has to shift from concentrating on the redistribution of wealth to promoting wealth creation. Rather than offering subsidies to business, government should foster conditions that lead firms to innovate and workers to become more efficient in the global economy.

The New Democrats also referred to the new progressivism as the third way, a term that eventually came to have preference over the former one. These ideas helped drive the policies that the successive Clinton administrations introduced, or aimed to introduce – among them fiscal discipline, health care reform, investment in education and training, welfare-to-work schemes, urban renewal programmes, and taking a hard line on crime and punishment. To them they added notions of active interventionism on the international scene.

Partly borrowing from the New Democrats, and partly following its own line of political evolution, the Labour Party in Britain converged on similar ideas. Under Tony Blair's leadership, the party broke with its own 'old progressivism' – Clause 4 of the Labour Party constitution. Blair started to refer to New Labour as developing a third way, eventually putting his name to a pamphlet of the same title.[2]

Over the past half-century, the document says, two forms of politics have dominated thinking and policy-making in most Western countries: 'a highly statist brand of social democracy' and right-wing, free-market philosophy (neoliberalism). Britain has experienced both of these in

[2] Tony Blair, *The Third Way*. London: Fabian Society, 1998.

full-blooded form, which is why the third way has special relevance there. Some neoliberal reforms were 'necessary acts of modernization'. Yet the neoliberals simply ignored the social problems produced by deregulated markets, which have created serious threats to social cohesion.

The New Democrats and New Labour have given particular attention to family life, crime, and the decay of community – a conscious attempt to relate policies of the left to what are seen as prime concerns of ordinary citizens. We need a third way approach to the family, distinct from those who simply ignore the issue on the one hand and those, on the other, who want to turn the clock back to a time before women went out to work. Changes in the family are related to antisocial behaviour and crime. Responding to anxieties about crime is seen as vital to third way policies: hence Tony Blair's celebrated statement that the left should be 'tough on crime and tough on the causes of crime'.

When New Labour first came into government, there was intense interest among social democratic parties in Continental Europe. Since that time, however, responses to the claim that the Labour Party is developing a new form of left-of-centre politics have been mixed. Some Continental social democratic leaders, having investigated what was on offer, found it distinctly underwhelming. Others have been more receptive. In April 1999, at the height of the Kosovo conflict, a public dialogue on third way politics was held in Washington.[3] Bill Clinton, Tony

---

[3] The White House, 'The third way: progressive governance for the 21st century' (25 April 1999).

Blair, Gerhard Schröder, Wim Kok – at that time prime minister of the Netherlands – and Massimo D'Alema, the Italian prime minister, attended.

There was considerable agreement among the Anglo-Saxon leaders and their Continental counterparts. Kok admitted that he liked the third way approach 'very much', but also felt that Dutch social democrats had already come to similar ideas and policies independently. Together with the Scandinavian countries, Holland is a country having one of the highest levels of social benefits. Yet in the current era, he agreed, it is not enough that people should be protected by government: they 'must also feel the urgency of responsibility', for 'you have rights, but also responsibilities'. In a world marked by rapid social and technological change, government must be empowering rather than heavy-handed.

D'Alema expressed similar sentiments. The European countries have developed strong systems of solidarity and protection. But these have become bureaucratic, and hence have 'slowed down development and limited the possibility of attaining success'. The third way suggests that it is possible to combine social solidarity with a dynamic economy, and this is a goal contemporary social democrats should strive for. To pursue it, we will need 'less national government, less central government, but greater governance over local processes', as well as opening out in the direction of the global community. Economic development will require lifelong learning and adaptation to new knowledge. 'Culture is the most important form of social inclusion, and I think we should invest in culture.' Such an approach, D'Alema concluded, has to break away from the old forms of welfare and social protection.

A short while after this meeting, Tony Blair and Gerhard Schröder published a joint paper entitled *Europe: The Third Way – die Neue Mitte*.[4] The paper seeks to provide a general framework for left-of-centre parties in Europe. 'The essential function of markets', the two leaders argue, 'must be complemented and improved by political action, not hampered by it.'

Blair and Schröder distance themselves decisively from what they define as the traditional social democratic outlook. The pursuit of social justice was often identified with a pre-eminent stress upon equality of outcome. As a consequence, effort and responsibility were ignored. Social democracy became associated with a dull conformity, rather than with creativity, diversity and achievement. Social justice was identified with ever higher levels of public spending almost regardless of what was actually achieved, or of the impact of taxation on competitiveness and job creation. Social benefits too often subdued enterprise as well as community spirit. Rights were elevated above responsibilities, resulting in a decline in mutual obligation and support.

Social democrats need a different approach to government, in which 'the state should not row, but steer: not so much control, as challenge'. The quality of public services must be improved and the performance of government monitored. A positive climate for entrepreneurial

---

[4] Tony Blair and Gerhard Schröder, *Europe: The Third Way – die Neue Mitte*. London: Labour Party and SPD, 1999.

independence and initiative has to be nurtured. Flexible markets are essential to respond effectively to technological change. Companies should not be inhibited from expanding by the existence of too many rules and restrictions. Modernizing social democrats, it is stressed, are not believers in *laisser-faire*. There has to be a newly defined role for an active state, which must continue to pursue social programmes. Employment and growth, however, cannot any longer be promoted by deficit spending. Levels of government borrowing should decrease rather than increase.

Critical reactions

Given its prominence in sources like these, and in shaping government policies in the US, UK and elsewhere, it is hardly surprising that the third way has sparked a variety of critical responses. Many, of course, come from conservative circles. Most right-wing critics see third way politics as either a mishmash of already familiar ideas and policies, or as lacking any distinguishable content at all. An article in *The Economist*, for instance, speaks of the third way's 'fundamental hollowness'. Trying to give an exact meaning to this political philosophy is 'like wrestling with an inflatable man. If you get a grip on one limb, all the hot air rushes to another.'[5]

I shall be more concerned with critical reactions com-

---

[5] 'Goldilocks politics.' *The Economist* (19 December 1998): 49 and 47.

ing from within the left. Many leftists agree with their conservative counterparts that the content of third way doctrines is elusive. They also stress the indebtedness of the third way programme to its supposed opponents, the free marketeers. The third way is seen as presenting an essentially right-wing philosophy in a somewhat more attractive light – Mrs Thatcher without a handbag.

The Anglo-Saxon critics

Jeff Faux, writing in an American context about the Democrats, is one of those who holds that the third way is 'an intellectually amorphous substance'; it has 'become so wide that it is more like a political parking lot than a highway to anywhere in particular'.[6] So much so, he continues, that the term has been applied to virtually every prominent political leader one can think of – not just Bill Clinton and Tony Blair, but 'Chrétien of Canada, Prodi of Italy, Jospin of France, Salinas and Zedillo of Mexico, Schröder of Germany, Cardoso of Brazil, Menem of Argentina – even Boris Yeltsin!'.

Faux distinguishes three claims in terms of which the third way should be judged: that it has a coherent analysis of the declining relevance of the 'old left'; that it provides an effective basis for rebuilding the fortunes of social democratic parties; and that it has a plausible strategy for dealing with issues of the post-Cold War age.

[6] Jeff Faux, 'Lost on the third way'. *Dissent* 46/2 (Spring 1999): 67–76, 75.

He accepts that what he calls the 'mainstream left' has to adapt to a world in rapid change. However, on each of the three issues just mentioned the third way has proved less than adequate. In the manner in which it developed in the US, at least, it was not originally constructed as a coherent political philosophy. The third way is not in fact a systematic approach at all, but developed as a tactical response to Democratic failures in the presidential elections of 1980 and 1984. The Clintonite Democrats claimed that because of its New Deal mentality the party was no longer in touch with the anxieties and aspirations of ordinary Americans. To become successful again in elections, the party had to respond to their concerns, and give priority to 'conservative' issues, such as law and order, rather than to questions of economic security. In particular, the New Democrats believed they had to break with a 'tax and spend' approach.

Faux disputes much of the historical ground on which these interpretations are based. Democratic presidents have cut taxes as often as they have raised them. Some Republican presidents, such as Ronald Reagan, have been more fiscally irresponsible than Democratic leaders – they wanted to spend on big government for purposes of defence, not, as the Democrats wanted, for social programmes. Moreover, in practice, the main proposals the New Democrats came up with were actually those which the 'mainstream left' had been advocating for a long while, such as more spending on education and child care.

It wasn't a new programme, Faux asserts, which lay behind the successful presidential campaigns of 1992 or 1996. The campaigns were fought mainly on the basis of the economy, and Bill Clinton won because of support from traditional Democratic groups – labour unions, minorities, and the poor. 'The lesson is that full employment beats conservative family values – just the opposite of the New Democrats' claim.'

The New Democrats, he says, have echoed the relentless complaints of the conservatives about over-sized government. As a result, they have acquiesced in a failure of government to stand out against the excesses of the market. The message that the Clintonite Democrats have sent to the average American facing the competition of the new global economy is: you're on your own. They have contributed to declining trust in government, rather than helping to reverse it.

The claim that third way thinking has fashioned a strategy effective in the new global economy, Faux declares, isn't persuasive. There is no new strategy, but in fact an old one. The third way expresses the world-view of the multinational corporate sector – that the global marketplace only works effectively if government plays a minimal role. The response has been a rising hostility to globalization. The free-flowing nature of global capital has outstripped the capability of international agencies to 'keep markets from self-destructing and to keep their people from suffering the brutal consequences'. Left-of-centre parties, the New Democrats say, should stop trying to guarantee outcomes for their citizens; all they can do is help provide opportunities for them to make the best of their lives. However, 'the new global economy, which the third way aggressively promotes, undercuts the third way premises every day'.

Third way thinking seeks to expand opportunities, but is silent about the unequal distribution of wealth and power. The third way has not proved to be a philosophy that moves political policy-making 'beyond left and right'. Instead, it is 'primarily a rationalization for political compromise *between* left and right, in which the left moves closer to the right'.

Comparable views have been expressed by critics writing in Britain. In December 1998, *Marxism Today* published a comprehensive attack upon New Labour, in a one-off special issue. The magazine had ceased regular publication some years before. The special issue had a picture of Tony Blair on the front. Printed across the picture in giant letters was the single word: 'Wrong'. Those involved all criticized New Labour for taking over too much from Thatcherism.

The main contribution was from the influential thinker Stuart Hall, entitled 'The great moving nowhere show'.[7] In the 1980s Hall developed a persuasive account of the nature of Thatcherism and the reasons for its success. Thatcherism was a radical doctrine, the aim of which was to alter the political landscape. Mrs Thatcher knew who she was against: 'she knew that, to achieve radical change, politics must be conducted like a war of position between adversaries. She clearly identified her enemies, remorselessly dividing the political field: Wets v Drys, Us v Them, those who are "with us" v "the enemy within".'

[7] Stuart Hall, 'The great moving nowhere show.' *Marxism Today* (November/December 1998): 9–14.

Tony Blair and New Labour claim to have a project at least as ambitious as Mrs Thatcher's. But in practice third way politics shies away from radicalism, opting for a middle course on everything. It advocates a 'politics without adversaries' and therefore ends up accepting the world as it is rather than truly seeking to transform it.

New Labour has succumbed to a sweeping view of globalization, which provides 'the dubious legitimacy' of the third way project. Globalization is treated as if it were an irresistible force of nature, as much outside our influence as the weather. New Labour has been seduced by the gospel that global markets are self-regulating and require no social or institutional framework to function. The sovereign consumer has replaced the ideas of the citizen and the public sphere.

The image that guides New Labour policies, Hall says, is one of the lonely individual, set free from the state in order to face life's risks alone – 'like those lean urban "survivors" on their mountain bikes who haunt our streets'. The social insurance of the welfare state was originally designed to underwrite citizenship – to bind rich and poor alike into society. Cutting back on public funding stigmatizes welfare recipients, and produces a two-tier system, where the better off buy themselves private provision for their needs.

Tony Blair's pamphlet on the third way is dismissed with some scorn. It acknowledges increasing inequalities, but offers no strategy for securing a more equitable distribution of income or wealth. No reference is made to power. Instead there is vague talk about the values of the left. What distinguishes a party of the left isn't its values, Hall argues, but a perennial dissatisfaction with markets.

Another British critic, Alan Ryan, offers a different interpretation of third way politics and its claims to originality.[8] The third way is a distinct and viable political position, he proposes, but it isn't an innovation. It first emerged in British politics about a century ago – at which point it was known as New Liberalism. 'The truth is that the third way is neither New Labour, as its admirers say, nor warmed over Thatcherism, as its detractors say, but a reversion to a very old idea.' The third way attempts to avoid an excessive domination of the state over social and economic life, but does not accept that the market can be left to its own devices. These were exactly the views held by the New Liberals. Even the anxieties and problems of the electorate, to which third way politics reacts, are similar to those of the turn of the century. Concerns about deteriorating education and rising crime rates echo the fears of the early 1900s.

The third way of today, Ryan continues, does not in fact have an effective response to these problems. It will fade away, as its forerunner did. It has no principled answer, for example, to rising unemployment, should a downswing in the economic cycle occur. At that point, a third way government would have to move either to the left or to the right – to raise taxes and borrow, or stick to a fiscally 'responsible' position, and see unemployment climb.

[8] Alan Ryan, 'Britain: recycling the third way.' *Dissent* 46/2 (Spring 1999): 77–80.

The Third Way and its Critics

The turn-of-the-century third way was actually in some respects superior to its more recent counterpart. The current version of third way politics is trying to reduce intervention in the marketplace in the face of the turbulent nature of the world economy, arguably the opposite of what we need; while in the areas of crime and education it has an unacceptably authoritarian standpoint. 'To the extent to which it is a coherent or acceptable approach to government, it resembles the New Liberalism of the beginning of the century; to the extent that it does not resemble it, it is neither coherent nor attractive.'

Continental responses

The Blair–Schröder paper passed almost without notice in the UK. In Germany, by contrast, it proved enormously controversial. Ex-finance minister Oskar Lafontaine launched a stinging attack on it and on the third way more generally. The third way, he declared, is no way at all – 'Der dritte Weg ist ein Holzweg'.[9]

The idea of 'modernization', Lafontaine says, comes down to little more than an endorsement of global free-market capitalism. The concept is reduced merely to economic categories. The questions of how we should live together, and of what sort of society we want, are declared irrelevant. Social democrats should have a different concept of 'the modern', one that stands in the tradition of the Enlightenment and which places as its

[9] Oskar Lafontaine, *Das Herz schlägt links*. Munich: Econ, 1999.

14

prime value the freedom of the individual. The left must fight against the intrusiveness of the market and against the insecurities the global economy brings in its train. Globalization is largely the result of political decisions to deregulate markets. As a result, the world economy has become a casino economy – save that, in this particular casino, ordinary people don't get to play. Their money is often involved – in the shape, for example, of pension funds. But it is banks, finance companies and other power brokers who take the decisions about what happens to it.

Financial markets, and those who dominate them, have to be subjected to regulation in order to put social goals above economic ones. In Europe we can also use other strategies to curb the influence of the world marketplace. The European Union can resist the worst features of the world economy and by keeping spending levels high can defend a 'social Europe'. Coordination of tax policies in the European Union will be necessary to achieve this end. It is this view, Lafontaine comments ironically, which led the *Sun* newspaper to call him 'the most dangerous man in Europe'. Lafontaine insists that 'not the "market", but democratically chosen governments and parliaments must take the decisions that determine the future of our society'.

A similar division between 'modernizers' and 'traditionalists' has opened up in many countries. Some critics from the left, however, take quite a different tack from Lafontaine. For them, the more advanced sectors of Continental social democracy already incorporate the worthwhile contributions the third way has to offer.

According to Erkki Tuomioja, writing from a Finnish context, the idea that third way prescriptions might be relevant to other European countries, such as the Nordic states, 'is baffling'.[10] Consider welfare reform, for example. Why should policies relevant to a British context have any bearing on more fully fledged welfare systems? After all, the UK is not a welfare state 'in any sense that is familiar to and accepted by most people in the Nordic countries'. Britain (in common with the US) has one of the highest levels of economic inequality of any of the developed societies.

Third way writers, Tuomioja says, call for reform of the welfare state because it hasn't been especially good at reducing inequalities. In fact, in the Nordic countries the welfare state 'has been extraordinarily successful in eliminating poverty'. Welfare states in northern Europe have mostly had a universalist approach to benefits and public services, in contrast to the Anglo-Saxon countries. As a result, most people share common experiences of public provision – there is both redistribution of income and increased social solidarity.

The Nordic welfare model involves civil society groups in the running of welfare services and allocates a high degree of local autonomy in so doing. Struggles over public ownership haven't had the central place they have in Britain. Finland is already in most respects a 'third way country'. Take the example of pensions. In Finland, there is a mixed system of pensions, with a state-provided uni-

[10] Erkki Tuomioja, 'Blairism may not work elsewhere in Europe.' Newsletter of the Finnish Institute in London (July 1998).

versal pension plus earnings-related pensions and controlled private sector provision.

Moreover, the Nordic welfare states have long since concentrated upon active labour market policies, now making a delayed appearance in an Anglo-Saxon context under the label of 'welfare to work'. Nordic social democracy has been characterized by a willingness to introduce reforms on a pragmatic basis with the aim of finding solutions that are effective. Advocates of third way politics suggest that a different orientation to politics is needed because existing social democratic policies have failed. 'This is something most European social democrats would not agree with. Reforms and new thinking are needed, not because of social democratic failure but because the lifetime full employment conditions of Fordist mass production and consumption and of Keynesianism-in-one-country on which the Nordic model was originally built do not exist any more.'

Tuomioja is not claiming, he stresses, that all is well with the Scandinavian welfare states. On the contrary, they face major problems. But they should be able to deal with these without structural changes that would bring them closer to the Anglo-American system. Unemployment, for example, remains high in Finland. Adjustments needed to reduce it can be made without changing the fundamental character of the Nordic social contract. Social democracy has always been able to implement reforms on a pragmatic basis, a more effective outlook than the search for 'an ephemeral third way'.

Another critic, Vicenç Navarro, comes to his assessment of the third way from a Spanish perspective.[11] Navarro recounts how, while acting as an adviser to the Spanish Socialist Party, he was asked to write an introduction to the Spanish translation of Blair's *Third Way* pamphlet. After looking at it, however, he declined, feeling it to be almost the opposite of what the European left needs. Third way politics supposedly develops a perspective beyond both old-style social democracy and neoliberalism. But this position, Navarro says, ignores the diverse nature of Continental social democracy. It also ignores the different forms of conservatism that exist in Europe and elsewhere. In Europe most conservative governments haven't taken a neoliberal line. Christian Democrats have long been suspicious of unfettered capitalism, and advocate a role – although a restricted one – for the state, as well as endorsing developed welfare institutions. Third way politics steals some of their clothes. In third way politics, 'there is more than a touch of Christian Democracy with a sprinkling of Liberal Party'.

Like the Christian Democrats, third way politics calls for a revival of civil society, which is threatened if the state grows too large. However, it is a mistake, Navarro argues, to suppose that the expansion of the state – at least, in its role as welfare state – undermines civil society. On the contrary, where countries have a well-funded welfare state, providing general benefits for the commu-

---

[11] Vicenç Navarro, 'Is there a third way?' Mimeo paper, Pompeu Fabra University, Barcelona (1999): 10. Navarro's arguments were subsequently published and further elaborated in 'La tercera via: un análisis critico.' *Claves de Razón Práctica* 96 (October 1999).

nity, they also have a developed civil society. Look, for example, at the areas of northern Italy led by left governments – public responsibility and a flourishing civil society go hand in hand. The third way, Navarro agrees with Tuomioja, 'might be new in the UK, but it is quite old in Europe'. 'Social democracy needs a process of reform, but not in a third way direction . . . What seems to be needed is not for social democracy to learn from the third way, but for the third way to learn from "classical" social democracy.'

The sociologist Ralf Dahrendorf once famously wrote of the 'end of the social democratic century'.[12] He still harbours suspicions about the revival of social democracy, especially in its third way guise. How could anyone, Dahrendorf asks rhetorically, who knew of its past choose to resurrect the term 'third way'? After all, 'third way' has a dubious history from Franco to Tito, quite often referring to anti-democratic forms of politics, especially those having corporatist or syndicalist goals.

In its current version, Dahrendorf asserts, third way politics is a project with Anglo-Saxon origins. What he calls 'the Giddens–Blair concept' of the third way is a largely unsuccessful attempt to develop a 'big idea' for our times. It is a politics that speaks of the need for hard choices, but then avoids them by trying to please everyone. There is a 'big question' that confronts us all today, Dahrendorf argues: 'how can we combine sustainable

[12] Ralf Dahrendorf, 'Whatever happened to liberty?' *New Statesman* (6 September 1999): 25–7. See also Dahrendorf, *Ein neuer Dritter Weg?* Tübingen: Mohr Siebeck, 1999.

prosperity with social solidarity, within institutions that guarantee liberty?' But there is no big answer.

There can't really be a coherent third way, Dahrendorf argues – only an array of different policy responses as we try to cope with a changing world. We face new questions, but we haven't got systematic solutions for them. For instance, reform of the welfare state is necessary, and this must mean a pulling back from universal benefits. How can this be done while still preserving social solidarity? No one really knows. Civil society should take over tasks which can't be effectively run by the state. But how this should be accomplished isn't easy to see, and all we can do is to deal with aspects of the issue. We have to find new ways of defending public space, and redraw the boundaries between public and private. Third way politics is in thrall to the market, but the public sphere is not one that can be provided for by markets. The market doesn't create safe neighbourhoods or clean streets and pathways.

Third way authors and politicians talk a lot about community, but they lose sight of the core importance of democratic freedoms. There is one word, Dahrendorf says, that hardly ever appears in publications by the promoters of the third way – liberty. This isn't accidental. For the third way isn't about open society or liberties. Echoing the comments of Alan Ryan, Dahrendorf argues that there is an 'authoritarian streak' in third way politics. 'I wonder whether the curious silence about the fundamental value of a decent life, liberty – old, very old liberty if you wish – will not involuntarily make this political episode one further element in a dangerous development.' So perhaps, obliquely, as Dahrendorf interprets it, third way politics does actually come back to the authoritarianism associated with the term in the past.

There is one final source of criticism of third way politics that deserves mention. This is the ecological critique. Al Gore, a key New Democratic figure, has written an important book about environmentalism.[13] Why, then, critics ask, haven't ecological concerns been more closely integrated with third way politics?

All politicians, of course, pay lip-service to environmental issues. Third way authors and politicians, it has been argued, are no different. How does an emphasis upon economic growth and the generating of jobs square with an ecological outlook? Social democrats have long had trouble introducing a serious strand of ecological thinking into their doctrines, and in this respect the third way seems more of the same. Thus the New Democrats in the US have had close ties with some of the large biotechnology companies, and appear to support their interests rather than putting ecological considerations first.

In the controversy about genetically modified foods in the UK, New Labour has refused to condemn the actions of such companies. It has been strongly criticized for so doing. Critics from within the green movement argue for a moratorium, or a complete ban, on such foods. Here there is a certain joining of hands with critics such as Faux and Hall. Third way politicians refuse to embrace a precautionary principle, critics from the green move-

---

[13] Al Gore, *Earth in the Balance*. London: Earthscan, 1992.

ment say, because they are reluctant to face up to corporate power.[14]

The critics: a summary

Since the commentators referred to come from different positions, a diversity of criticisms is offered by them. The critical observations can be grouped, however, into a limited range of categories. It is argued that the third way:

(1) Is an amorphous political project, difficult to pin down and lacking direction. Since it isn't clear who or what third way politicians are against, it is hard to say what they are for. The very name 'third way' is perhaps indicative of this fuzziness, since it has such a chequered history, and has been used so often before. 'Third way' is empty of content because it is defined only negatively, as contrasted to old-style social democracy and neoliberalism. Any worthwhile political perspective should surely be capable of more active definition. By implication other perspectives, closer either to the traditional left or to the neoliberal right, are more coherent and more capable of responding effectively to political issues in current times.

(2) Fails to sustain the proper outlook of the left and hence, whether deliberately or not, lapses into a form of conservatism. The advocates of the third way define

[14] See, for instance, Ian Willmore, 'Environment: sun sets on a greener future.' *Guardian* (23 July, 1997).

themselves as 'centre-left', but in fact have simply moved towards the right. A preoccupation with the political centre is manifestly not compatible with the goals of the left. Stuart Hall condemns New Labour, for example, for its preoccupation with 'middle England' – middle-class voters, located mainly in the south of the country, rather than the less prosperous north. This orientation, Hall says, is 'profoundly traditionalist and backward looking'. Manual workers, the backbone of support for a leftist party, slip out of view. When Alan Ryan says the views of third way politicians today are the same as those of the New Liberals of yesteryear, he is making much the same point. The New Liberals sought a middle-of-the-road position. They accepted some leftist values, but distanced themselves firmly from most versions of socialism.

The conservatism of the third way is also said to appear in its views of the family and the control of crime. Third way politicians want to defend the traditional family, while placing more emphasis than most on the left have done upon personal responsibility for criminal behaviour, and hence upon firm policing. Aren't these again the policies of the right? These attitudes underlie Dahrendorf's feeling that third way politics allocates too little place for individual liberties.

(3) Accepts the basic framework of neoliberalism, especially as concerns the global marketplace. Globalization and the information revolution are quite rightly fastened upon by the critics as key concerns of third way politics. According to them, however, the third way takes

globalization as a given. Crucially, it fails to contest inequalities of income, wealth and power.

This is easily the most common criticism that those on the more traditional left make of the third way 'modernizers'. Globalization producers winners and losers. Third way offers nothing to the losers – it cannot do so, because it adopts the world-view of the winners. Redistribution, always one of the major aims of the left, seems to have been discarded. Promoting greater equality is impossible without using the state to redress the inequities created by the market. In wanting to limit the role of government and the state, the third way is again accepting one of the main themes of the neoliberals, with their wish to reduce the scope of state power. There is no need to worry about government getting too large. As Navarro says, state and civil society are not mutually exclusive.

(4) Is essentially an Anglo-Saxon project, bearing the hallmarks of the societies in which it originated. The term 'third way' has been resurrected by politicians and intellectuals in countries that have only weakly developed welfare systems, and where inequalities are more marked than elsewhere. Policies developed in such a context are of little use to societies that are further along the road to social justice and more comprehensive welfare provision.

The importing of third way ideas into such contexts would be a retrograde step. In so far as the third way does have anything relevant to more highly evolved welfare states, the policies involved are familiar to social democrats anyway. Active labour market policies, for instance, were established in Sweden well before they were heard of in the US or UK.

(5)   Has no distinctive economic policy, other than allowing the market to rule the roost. Old-style social democracy had a coherent economic strategy, based upon state intervention in the marketplace, demand management and full employment. The neoliberals also had a clear policy outlook – privatization and the deregulation of markets would supposedly benefit everyone, rich and poor alike. Third way economic thinking veers more towards the latter rather than the former, but lacks any distinctive policy orientations of its own.

Having no definite economic thinking, it is argued, third way politics is liable to succumb to drift. The US economy might have been remarkably successful in recent years, but this seems to have nothing much to do with the activities of government policy. The third way, as Alan Ryan puts it, has been riding a wave of economic prosperity: it has no way of coping should there be an economic turndown.

(6)   In common with its two main rivals, has no effective way of coping with ecological issues, save for giving token recognition to them. In accepting globalization, third way politics acquiesces in the destructive consequences that world economic development has for the environment. By endorsing technological change, the third way demonstrates its indifference to ecological damage. Scientific and technological development today is largely driven by big business, which will always put profit ahead of environmental considerations. The connection between

the large corporations and scientific innovation is much more worrying than it used to be, given the profound nature of the scientific discoveries now being made, such as those in the field of the life sciences. The only means of approaching such developments, many ecological authors say, is through a precautionary outlook. We should rein back scientific innovation until we are sure of its likely consequences.

2

Social Democracy and the Third Way

Dahrendorf asks, why speak of the 'third way', given that the term has been so often employed in earlier times, and has questionable origins? In response to this query, it should be emphasized that nothing in fact does hang on the term itself.[1] Others can be substituted – in this text I shall use 'the modernizing left' and 'modernizing social democracy' as synonyms for it. I believe 'third way' is worth keeping, however, because it has become much more widely established today than it ever was before.

Third way politics is above all an endeavour to respond to change. In the 1980s, during the same period in which he worked out his interpretation of Thatcherism, Stuart Hall formulated an analysis of 'New Times' that foresaw a necessary transformation of socialist politics. A new era is arriving marked by a shift from manufacturing production to information technology, the declining role of

---

[1] Anthony Giddens, *The Third Way: The Renewal of Social Democracy*. Cambridge: Polity Press, 1998, pp. 24–6.

27

class politics and the expansion of choice in consumption, lifestyle and sexuality.[2] New Times meant that the whole legacy of socialist and social democratic thought would have to be recast.

Yet Hall's own political formulae, in so far as they are spelled out at all, appear to repeat unchanged the doctrines of the traditional left. Left-of-centre politics, he says, is above all concerned with collective provision to counter the inequalities and instabilities produced by markets. Capitalism is the problem, and the aim of the left should be to beef up the state and its tax revenues in order to control it and its *agents provocateurs*, the large corporations.

But this is to act as though New Times never existed. New Times and Old Left don't and can't belong together. The objective of third way politics, as I would see it, is to carry through the political implications of New Times, recognizing that this means that the established positions and policies of the left have to be profoundly revised. If social democrats are to have real purchase on the world, their doctrines have to be rethought as radically as half a century ago, when social democracy originally broke away from Marxism.

Post-1989 we can't think of left and right in the same way as many once did. Nor can social democrats any longer see either capitalism or markets as the source of most of the problems that beset modern societies. Government and the state are at the origin of social problems

[2] Stuart Hall and Martin Jacques, *New Times*. London: Lawrence & Wishart, 1989.

as well as markets. Third way politics also looks to build upon a core lesson of 1989 and after – the fact that a strong civil society is necessary both for effective democratic government and for a well-functioning market system.

I propose to turn the arguments of the critics on their head. Third way politics – modernizing social democracy – can develop a political programme that is integrated and robust. Far from displacing social justice and solidarity, third way politics, I shall argue, represents the only effective means of pursuing these ideals today. Far from being unable to deal with questions of inequality and corporate power, it is the only approach able to do so in the context of the contemporary world. The Blair–Schröder paper could quite easily have made this point and developed it. It is unfortunate that it did not.

Third way politics does not neglect the public realm: it offers the means of reconstructing and renewing public institutions, which is one of its prime objectives. Moreover, rather than simply accepting globalization as a given, the third way suggests policies that respond to it in a sophisticated fashion. Alternative views of globalization, including those of the old left critics, aren't up to the task. The debate about globalization is deeply bound up with ecological issues and problems. Instead of treating these as a side issue, third way politics sees them as fundamental to the new political concerns. The main difference between the old and the modernizing left isn't that the one preserves leftist values whereas the other has abandoned them. It is that advocates of third way politics argue that far more revision is needed in social democratic doctrines to sustain those values than the old left allows.

The term 'third way' might have been reintroduced into politics from an Anglo-Saxon context, but I want to argue strongly that third way politics is not a distinctively Anglo-Saxon project. Tuomioja is entirely correct to point out that some of the policies of the New Democrats and New Labour were developed earlier on the Continent. Since the mid-1980s, major policy changes have been made by many Continental social democratic parties – and by most others in different parts of the world. Neoliberalism did not replace other forms of conservatism in continental Europe, yet it was everywhere in the ideological vanguard. On the Continent as in the US and Britain social democrats were concerned to react to its claims. As they did so, and sought to resist the neoliberal challenge, they found it necessary to move away from their earlier positions and policies.

Those who were constructing a new point of departure for the Labour Party in the UK were conscious of these parallels. The welfare-to-work schemes, for example, that are a major feature of Labour Party policy drew not only upon the American experience, but upon the Continental one too. One of the main figures involved in shaping welfare-to-work policy in the UK, the economist Richard Layard, based his ideas as much on Swedish policies as upon those coming from the US.[3]

There are many other convergent developments. The

[3] Richard Layard, *How To Beat Unemployment*. Oxford: Oxford University Press, 1998.

welfare and labour market reforms introduced in Denmark in 1993–4 differ significantly from those in Britain, but there are big areas of overlap. The Danish 'negotiated economy', the much-discussed 'polder model' in the Netherlands, and many other changes going on in Continental social democracy are of direct relevance to third way politics. The modernizing of social democracy is an ongoing process, and different countries are coming to it from different starting-points and with varying types of policy innovation.

Some have suggested that a number of different 'third ways' can be distinguished. A recent work of the Basic Values Commission of the German Social Democratic Party, for instance, distinguishes four different 'third ways' in Europe.[4] One is the 'market-oriented' approach taken by New Labour. The Dutch approach is 'market- and consensus-oriented'. Sweden is treading the path of the 'reformed welfare state', retaining a good deal of continuity with its past. Continuity of development is also apparent in France, which is sticking to the 'state-led way'. However, I think it would be more accurate to speak of a single broad stream of third way thinking, to which the various parties and governments are contributing.

Third way politics, as I understand it here at any rate, is an attempt to carry further the reform processes social democrats have already begun, and offers a framework within which those processes can be put. The New Democrats and New Labour have much to contribute to this

---

[4] Grundwertekommission beim Parteivorstand der SPD, *Dritte Weg –Neue Mitte*. Berlin, 1999.

endeavour. Having experienced neoliberal government in 'full-blooded form' is one of the reasons for this. The electoral successes of Ronald Reagan and Mrs Thatcher led the left, or some on the left, in the US and UK to be more prepared to question orthodoxies than their counterparts in countries where there had not been long periods of neoliberal rule.

Social democracy has had to transform itself to survive, but social democrats must be prepared to innovate even more if they are to prosper. The structural changes to which all political parties must adapt are far-reaching. In what follows, I shall not identify third way politics with the policy programme of any particular party or country. Rather, I shall be concerned to flesh out what a framework for left-of-centre politics can be in the contemporary age, concentrating particularly on the problem areas referred to by the critics. Just as the American new progressives originally argued, the third way implies a thorough-going programme of policy modernization. It looks to modernize the state and government, including the welfare state, plus the economy and other sectors of society. 'Modernization' here means reforming social institutions to meet the demands of a globalizing information order. It is certainly not to be identified solely with economic development.

Third way politics is not a continuation of neoliberalism, but an alternative political philosophy to it. Social democrats, as I shall emphasize below, need to overcome some of their worries and fears about markets. But the neoliberal idea that markets should almost everywhere stand in place of public goods is ridiculous. Neoliberalism is a deeply flawed approach to politics, because it supposes that no responsibility needs to be taken for the social consequences of market-based decisions. Markets can't even function without a social and ethical framework – which they themselves cannot provide. Neither trickle-down effects, nor a minimal welfare state, are able to provide the social goods that a decent society must involve.

Yet it won't do, as writers from the old left suggest, merely to counterpose the state to markets. Markets do not always increase inequality, but can sometimes be the means of overcoming it. Moreover, while active government is needed to promote egalitarian policies, the left has to learn to recognize that the state itself can produce inequality, as well as having other counter-productive effects on individuals' lives – even when it is recognizably democratic and motivated by good intentions. Even in its most developed forms, the welfare state was never an unalloyed good. All welfare states create problems of dependency, moral hazard, bureaucracy, interest-group formation and fraud.

To argue that the New Democrats and New Labour have pioneered some key ideas and policies of third way politics does not imply taking the US or the UK as models for Continental social democrats to aspire to. Both countries have public institutions and infrastructures inferior to those of many Continental countries. With some important qualifications to be discussed later, each has unacceptably high levels of economic inequality. But we cannot go on to argue, as Tuomioja seems to think, that the more advanced welfare states can rest on their laurels. In the absence of further reform, they are likely to be more vulnerable to the changes now happening than countries 'further back' on the welfare scale.

The left and the market

Many on the more traditional left would accept Hall's view that the left is defined by its concern with the dangers of market, whose excesses need constantly to be reined back by the state. Today, however, this idea has become archaic. The left has to get comfortable with markets, with the role of business in the creation of wealth, and the fact that private capital is essential for social investment. The reformist left has long accepted that markets have a role alongside government, but the admission has in the past characteristically been a grudging one. As one observer has put it, the left still sought 'to replace the fundamentals of a market economy with centralised government control; to replace market competition with strategic protection; to replace the price mechanism with industry plans; and to replace market-driven profits with the largesse of public subsidies and special deals'.[5]

In the wake of the dissolution of communism, no one any longer argues for the banning of markets from most areas of the economy. It is hard even to remember that this was so widely thought of as a sensible and even ne-

[5] Mark Latham, 'Economic policy and the third way.' *Australian Economic Review* 31/4 (1998): 384–98, 392.

cessary aim. Yet since many on the left still harbour such profound doubts about markets, it is worth pointing out what markets do achieve.

Markets have, or can have, beneficial outcomes that go beyond productive efficiency. A successful market economy has an important 'hidden curriculum'. If adequately regulated, market exchange is essentially peaceful. Market relations have often been imposed by the use of force. Yet once a working market economy has been established, people who stand in exchange relationships have little cause to resort to it. 'Gangster capitalism', where rent-seeking is backed by the use of violence, is a specifically abnormal and unstable form of market structure.

In addition, market relations allow free choices to be made by consumers, at least where there is competition between multiple producers. In spite of the influence of advertising and other attempts by producers to shape tastes and needs, such choice is real. Markets can also favour attitudes of responsibility, since participants need to calculate the likely outcomes of what they do, whether they are producers or consumers. This factor helps explain other aspects of the liberating potential of markets, since the decisions the individual makes aren't given by authoritarian command or by bureaucracy.

A successful market economy generates far greater prosperity than any rival system. In effect, there is no rival system in place any longer, save in the residues of post-communist economies. A prime reason for the economic success of market exchange is that market mechanisms provide continuous signals for producers, traders and consumers. The command economies weren't able to provide for these continuous adjustments.

Accepting all this doesn't imply following a neoliberal line. Excessive dependence on market mechanisms has to be avoided for clear reasons. Markets respond to the desires of consumers, but as they do so can compromise other wants or needs. Markets can breed a commercialism that threatens other life values. Without external controls, markets have no restraining mechanisms – there is nothing in market exchange that limits what might be marketed. In addition, ethical standards, or standards of taste, have to be brought from the outside – from a public ethics, guaranteed in law.

Combined with entrepreneurial energy, a market economy is vastly more dynamic than any other type of economic system. Yet that very dynamism, intrinsic to wealth creation, generates major social costs that markets themselves don't meet – such as the social disruption caused by job loss as a result of economic slump or technological change. Nor can markets nurture the human capital they themselves require – government, families and communities have to do so. Market economies generate externalities, whose social implications have to be dealt with by other means. Environmental damage, for instance, can't be dealt with purely by market mechanisms.

Finally, markets aren't self-regulating. Their tendency to cyclical fluctuation needs to be limited by outside intervention, as does their tendency to create monopoly. The two are related, since in times of economic difficulty firms may try to merge or consolidate. However, monopoly also comes from the competitive process itself.

Economic actors often seek to set up monopolies or cartels because these protect them against potentially dangerous rivals. External agencies are needed to enforce competitiveness.

In his *Peddling Prosperity* Paul Krugman called one of his chapters 'In the Long Run Keynes is Still Alive'.[6] The slogan is an apt one. The decline of neoliberalism as a political philosophy has gone along with the receding influence of the economic theories that inspired it. The ideas of the new Keynesians allow us to make more sense of how the modern economy works, particularly at its cutting edge, the global financial economy. Suboptimal consequences can happen in any market sector as a result of the interaction of imperfectly competitive markets with the less than rational actions of individuals. In some situations, such as those found in the finance markets, the consequences can be extreme. The tendency of financial markets towards crisis is structural and needs to be coped with by collaborative intervention.

Adversaries and enemies

Whatever policies individual governments may follow, third way politics as a matter of principle must not be complacent or collusive in the face of power. There are interest groups, and groups of the powerful, that any self-respecting left-of-centre government must confront, face down, or regulate. The struggle to sustain and extend

[6] Paul Krugman, *Peddling Prosperity*. New York: Norton, 1995.

democratic mechanisms, control corporate power, and protect cultural minorities is fundamental to the third way, as it has been to previous forms of social democracy.

We must be careful, however, to separate these concerns from the 'politics of redemption' which lingers on among those on both the old left and the neoliberal right. The politics of the traditional left was – and is – grounded in finding and confronting the 'bad guys' – the adversaries, as Stuart Hall calls them. The bad guys are the capitalists, markets, the large corporations, the rich, or the US with its imperialist ambitions. The right, of course, has its own collection of bad guys – big government, cultural relativists, the poor, immigrants and criminals. Neutralize or get rid of the bad guys and all will be well. But there isn't a concentrated source of the ills of the world; we have to leave behind the politics of redemption.

We must also leave behind the idea that left and right is the sole and sovereign dividing-line in politics. Left and right certainly won't disappear, but the division between them has less compelling power than it used to do. In the absence of a redemptive model, to be on the left is indeed primarily a matter of values. It won't do to define the left in terms of its hostility to markets.

Just what the values of the left are, and how they differ from those of the right, have themselves been matters of long-standing debate. The most persuasive writer on the issue in recent years, however, Norberto Bobbio, sets them out in the following way.[7] To be on the left is to be

---

[7] Norberto Bobbio, *Left and Right*. Cambridge: Polity Press, 1996.

concerned with reducing inequality – more positively defined, with the pursuit of social justice. Other left values, such as social cooperation and protection of the vulnerable, stem from that abiding concern.

In these terms, third way politics is unequivocally a politics of the left. But just where the line should be drawn between left and right has shifted, and there are many political problems and issues that don't fit clearly into a left/right dimension. It is a fundamental mistake to attempt to cram them all into it. The division between left and right reflected a world where it was widely believed that capitalism could be transcended, and where class conflict shaped a good deal of political life. Neither of these conditions pertains today. 'Radicalism' cannot any longer be equated with 'being on the left'. On the contrary, it often means breaking with established leftist doctrines where they have lost their purchase on the world.

Take as a mundane example the debate about pensions. In considering pension reform, questions of social justice and protection are highly important: how can we ensure that older people don't live in poverty? How can welfare systems best be designed to provide care for the elderly and infirm? Yet many of the most important issues about ageing have nothing to do with social justice, and thinking radically about pensions involves placing these in the foreground.[8] Ageing is a much more diverse and actively shaped process than it used to be – in common with other areas of life in a globalizing era, what it

[8] Peter G. Peterson, *Gray Dawn*. New York: Random House, 1999.

is to be an 'older person' is more open and negotiable. Even the body doesn't passively 'age' any longer, but can be influenced by habits, diet and a person's approach to life.

Thinking radically about ageing means considering, for instance, whether pensions, or fixed ages of retirement, should exist *at all*. Pensions, after all, are an invention of the welfare state, and they are essentially only a form of savings. Why shouldn't older people have a statutory right to work? The expectation that older people have to be cared for by the state arguably creates a culture of dependency as noxious as any other.

These questions, like so many others we have to deal with today, are about 'life politics', rather than the 'emancipatory politics' of the left.[9] Life politics is about how we should respond to a world in which tradition and custom are losing their hold over our lives, and where science and technology have altered much of what used to be 'nature'. These transformations nearly all raise value or ethical questions, but not only to do with social justice. Ageing is a good case in point. We have to consider problems such as what the proper role of older people should be in a society where ageing is changing its meaning, what should be the relationship between the generations and a diversity of other issues.

The fact that left and right count for less than they used to do is also borne out by attitude surveys investigating the views of the electorate. 'New Times' are very

---

[9] Anthony Giddens, *Beyond Left and Right*. Cambridge: Polity Press, 1994.

evident here. In the industrial countries, and to some extent world-wide, what some political scientists call a 'new political culture' is arising in response to social and economic change. The new political culture diverges from the traditional model of class politics. It was this latter model that shaped socialism and social democracy, and which was the basis of traditional conceptions of capital and wage-labour.

Terry Nichols Clark lists a number of features of the new political culture, disclosed by research in a large range of industrial societies, including the EU countries, the US, Japan and Australasia.[10]

(1)   The left/right division in citizens' eyes too has become more a difference of values than of concerns about issues such as control of the means of production, or the role of government in social reform. Fiscal and social questions are explicitly distinguished from each other, such that citizens' views on the former cannot be deduced from their ideas about the latter. As class politics is replaced by the new political culture, belief in government intervention in economic life, on the one hand, and social attitudes, on the other, diverge. More people than before are against 'too much' government intervention in their lives, yet support other aspects of a 'leftist' agenda, especially on issues of personal and sexual freedom.

(2)   In the new political culture, 'market liberalism', which used to be associated with parties of the right, goes

---

[10] Terry Nichols Clark and Vincent Hoffman-Martinot, *The New Political Culture*. Boulder, CO: Westview, 1998.

41

along with 'social progressiveness' – once thought of as belonging to the left. New combinations of policy preferences come from these changing alignments. As affluence increases, lifestyle issues grow in importance as compared to economic or fiscal concerns – more so among the better-off, but also among poorer groups too. Lifestyle acts as a 'filter' for economic concerns. Security of employment, for instance, is seen as less important than it was; how much a particular type of job fits with wider aspirations counts for more than it did.

(3) The new political culture is sceptical of large bureaucracies and opposes political clientelism. Many citizens see local and regional government as able to meet their needs more effectively than the national state. They support an increasing role for non-profit voluntary agencies in the delivery of public services. Hierarchy is viewed with suspicion, as are traditional symbols and trappings of power.

(4) The new political culture is more widespread among younger people, the more educated and the more affluent, but is becoming the outlook of the majority. Socio-economic divisions tend to concentrate more than they did upon a separation between cosmopolitan social groups and inward-looking communities, where people either maintain more traditional class attitudes or feel largely alienated from the political process. The new political culture is as observable in European societies with strong traditions of social democracy, such as Scandinavia, as in the US or UK.

(5) Such changes in attitudes, which create a much larger pool of 'uncommitted' voters than used to exist,

reflect profound transformations in class structure. Only a generation ago, 40–50% of the labour force in the industrial societies was in manual jobs, concentrated in the manufacturing sector. Now that sector comprises less than 20% of the workforce in most countries, and the proportion is still falling. The class relations that used to be so closely bound up with political divisions between left and right are disappearing from view.

These findings stand behind the concern of third way politics with the political centre. To those who believe that all political problems divide into left and right, the centre is uninteresting – it is the neutral ground between clearly defined positions on either side. A politics that appeals to the centre is bound to be a politics of compromise. When third way politicians talk of moving to the centre, or of 'the new middle', those on the more traditional left respond with some derision. In particular, they ridicule the suggestion that there can be a 'radical centre' or an 'active middle'.

Stuart Hall speaks dismissively of New Labour's attempt to reach 'middle England', but doing so was the condition of the victory the party achieved. It did not happen at the expense of Labour's heartland constituencies, as Hall implies – its majorities in those areas increased. Moreover, current research shows that middle-class groups are by no means 'traditionalist'. The middle class is becoming internally heterogeneous. Those groups who tend to be most closely identified with the new political culture are 'wired workers' – the increasingly large 'infotech' sector of the middle class. Wired workers are people who work with computers most of the day, in non-hierarchical settings, and who are involved in problem-solving activities rather than repetitive tasks. According to some estimates, they now make up about a third of the workforce in the EU countries, and an even higher proportion in the US.

A concern for the centre should not be naively interpreted, as the critics do, as a forgoing of radicalism or the values of the left. Many policies that can quite properly be called radical transcend the left/right divide. They demand, and can be expected to get, cross-class support – policies in areas, for example, such as education, welfare reform, the economy, ecology and the control of crime. If social democrats cannot successfully address these issues – especially in the context of globalization and technological change – their electoral victories will be temporary ones. A basic question, of course, is: are such policies compatible with improving the lot of the underprivileged? I believe they are, for reasons to be given later.

Third way politics and moral conservatism

The 'original third way politicians', Bill Clinton and Tony Blair, have gone out of their way not to appear soft on crime. In addition, they speak up strongly for the family. In both the United States and Britain, single mothers have been targeted for welfare-to-work schemes. Tony Blair has said that, all things being equal, the two-parent family is the best social environment in which to bring up children. Does all this, as the critics assert, add up to an assault on liberty and tolerance?

I don't believe so – at least, again, as a matter of principle. We need to escape from the one-sided views of regulation held by the traditional left and by the neoliberals alike. Those on the old left favour heavy state intervention in economic life, but take quite a different approach to areas such as the family and sexuality. In these spheres, individuals should be free to follow their own inclinations. In the case of crime, they have tended to trace its causes to inequality or poverty, playing down the influence of personal responsibility. The neoliberals hold a reverse view. According to them, the state should withdraw from interference with the economy as much as possible, since the effect of state intervention is to distort otherwise rational market processes. So far as non-economic activity is concerned, however, strong regulation is necessary, because of the need to protect traditional morality. Crime comes from a decline in moral standards, brought about by rising individualism in personal life.

Economic regulation, moral anarchy; economic anarchy, strong moral controls – neither combination makes much sense. Government needs to play a regulative role across the board. In the area of family, for instance, it won't do simply to 'let a thousand flowers bloom'. Family policy needs to be aimed at promoting full sexual equality in the domestic sphere, protecting the interests of children, and helping to stabilize family life. Third way thinking in the area of the family does not, or should not, favour traditionalism or conservatism. The controversies between conservative advocates of the traditional family and those on the left who celebrate diversity have been unfruitful. In the industrial countries, family life has changed so much that there can be no route back to the traditional family as it is ordinarily understood. The theme of modernization has just as much application here as elsewhere. To accept this is not to endorse the idea that we need have no worries about the state of the family. Helen Wilkinson points out that

> there has been an unhealthy polarisation between liberals who affirm individualism, and tend to take a relativistic view of family values and structures, and conservatives who talk a lot about values but neglect household economies. The result? A policy impasse. Yet we have been presented with a false choice. Problems being experienced by families today are rooted both in economic stress (whether of time or money) and in family disintegration. Any progressive family policy must address both these issues or it will fail.[11]

The position developed by the New Democrats in the US marked an important contribution in this context. The Democrats used social research to reorient the family values debate. Many parents are working while at the same time coping with domestic responsibilities. Most recognize that such a balancing act cannot be carried on

---

[11] Helen Wilkinson, 'The family way: navigating a third way in family policy.' In *Tomorrow's Politics: The Third Way and Beyond*, ed. Ian Hargreaves and Ian Christie. London: Demos, 1998, pp. 112–25, 112.

within traditional family structures. They are worried about the instability of marriage and relationships, particularly its effects on children. These worries are backed up by research – for instance, other things being equal, children on average do in fact fare better in two-parent families.

Sarah McLanahan and Gary Sandefur drew together material from four national surveys and more than a decade of investigation in the US and other industrial countries. They concluded that the evidence is quite clear: 'Children who grow up in a household with only one biological parent are worse off, on average, than children who grow up in a household with both of their biological parents, regardless of the parents' race or educational background, regardless of whether the parents are married when the child is born, and regardless of whether the resident parent remarries.'[12] When they started their study, the researchers anticipated that the negative effects of single parenthood were really due to poverty and racial discrimination. The results showed this assumption to be only partly true.

Governments must respond to findings such as these. Social policy for the family, as for the economy, has to be predominantly 'supply side'. It should foster conditions in which individuals are able to form stable ties with others, especially where children are involved and accept the responsibilities that come along with contemporary freedoms. Many of the emphases of third way

[12] Sarah McLanahan and Gary Sandefur, *Growing Up With a Single Parent*. Cambridge, MA: Harvard University Press, 1994.

politics appear in a very direct way in family policy. In creating family-friendly work environments, making possible various forms of paid family leave, and in creating or sustaining high-quality child care, business and third sector groups can play key roles. Such programmes need often to be located in the communities with which they are concerned, as well as designed and run by local community agencies.

Policies aimed at the reduction of crime also need to be integrated with community renewal programmes and with community policing. Yet there's no point pretending that long-term strategies for reducing crime absolve us from dealing with criminality in the here and now. Third way politicians are right to point to the hypocrisy of the traditional left on this question. For a long time, many on the left denied the reality of crime, or sought to attribute criminality to other social problems. The work of the criminologists from the 'left realism school' changed all that. Many of the worries people have about crime are real and sensible and they need short-term solutions for them.[13]

In the UK, for example, crime rose over the period 1960–75, at a time of full employment and rising living standards. It has continued to climb since then. Crimes recorded by the police, the measure often used, are a notoriously unreliable indicator. However, other measures, such as the British Crime Survey, also showed that crime was on the increase – and that the real volume of crime is much higher than official police figures indicate.

[13] See Jock Young, *The Exclusive Society*. London: Sage, 1999.

Some studies in the UK show that half of respondents are victims of some form of crime at least once during the course of a year. These findings suggest that crime is a normal part of people's experience rather than an exceptional event. Some of the most serious crimes – violence and sexual assault – are much more common than was previously believed.

Rather than avoiding the issue of liberty, it should be placed at the forefront in discussing how to tackle crime through community initiatives. Where the lines are drawn between freedom and regulation is bound to be controversial. When the lives of local families are made miserable by racist groups of youths, would a street curfew after a certain hour add to the sum of available liberties or not? Should we try experimenting, as some have suggested, with urban safety zones in inner-city areas, where surveillance and saturation policing might create public spaces in which people could associate with each other? How far could and should electronic tagging replace conventional imprisonment or probation? However these questions are answered, the idea of substantive liberty is what matters – how far regulating some sorts of freedoms produces a net increase in freedom for communities as a whole.

Substantive freedom, I shall suggest in a later chapter, should be linked to social capability – to the positive capacity of individuals to contribute to their well-being and self-fulfilment. This in turn presumes a preoccupation with opportunity and, more specifically, equality of opportunity.

The New Democrats and New Labour stand accused

of moving their parties to the right. What they have done, however, is to begin to accommodate to the changes that limit the relevance of the old ideologies. They have shown that the left should listen to the anxieties that worry ordinary citizens. The traditional left's indifference to issues such as crime and family breakdown damaged its credibility in other areas where its policies were strong. Social democrats outside the Anglo-Saxon sphere shouldn't imagine these concerns are irrelevant to them. They are reflected in most Continental countries in the growth of the new parties and in the rise of the far right. Social democrats have to find a language to address these common concerns. The New Democrats and New Labour have demonstrated that 'once the left is credible on issues where it has traditionally been suspect . . . voters are willing to listen to it on issues such as education, health and the environment where they have a natural affinity for its positions'.[14]

Third way politics

The fundamentals of third way politics, as I would see them, can now be briefly stated. The third way:

(1)   Accepts the logic of '1989 and after' – that while left and right still count for a good deal in contemporary politics, there are many issues and problems that this

---

[14] Robert Philpot, 'Why Bill Clinton is a hero.' *New Statesman* (19 July 1999): 21.

opposition no longer helps illuminate. The attention which the third way gives to the political centre stems from this fact. This emphasis is wholly compatible with the claim that third way politics should involve radical policies.

(2)   Argues that the three key areas of power – government, the economy, and the communities of civil society – all need to be constrained in the interests of social solidarity and social justice. A democratic order, as well as an effective market economy, depends upon a flourishing civil society. Civil society, in turn, needs to be limited by the other two.

The sociologist Claus Offe points to six fallacies that a sophisticated political theory must avoid – each of which we have, or should have, learned a lot about through the experience of the past few decades.[15] The state can become too large and overextended – the neoliberals were right about this. But where the state is too confined, or loses its legitimacy, major social problems develop too. The same applies to markets. A society that allows the market to infiltrate too far into other institutions will experience a failure of public life. One that finds insufficient space for markets, however, will not be able to generate economic prosperity. Similarly, where the communities in civil society become too strong, democracy

---

[15] Claus Offe, 'The present historical transformation and some basic design options for societal institutions.' Paper presented at the seminar on 'Society and the Reform of the State', São Paulo (26–9 March 1998). I draw on Offe's discussion in this and other chapters.

as well as economic development can be threatened. Yet if the civic order is too weak, effective government and economic growth are put at risk.

(3) Proposes to construct a new social contract, based on the theorem 'no rights without responsibilities'. Those who profit from social goods should both use them responsibly, and give something back to the wider social community in return. Seen as a feature of citizenship, 'no rights without responsibilities' has to apply to politicians as well as citizens, to the rich as well as the poor, to business corporations as much as the private individual. Left-of-centre governments should be prepared to act upon it in all these areas.

(4) In the economic sphere, looks to develop a wide-ranging supply-side policy, which seeks to reconcile economic growth mechanisms with structural reform of the welfare state. In the new information economy, human (and social) capital becomes central to economic success. The cultivation of these forms of capital demands extensive social investment – in education, communications and infrastructure. The principle 'wherever possible invest in human capital' applies equally to the welfare state – which needs to be reconstructed as a 'social investment state'.

The creation of a 'new mixed economy' depends on a balance of regulation and deregulation, nationally and transnationally. The old left attributes many of the world's problems to the activities of business corporations. Corporate power certainly needs to be controlled by government and by international legislation. Yet when no one knows of any viable alternative to a market economy, demonizing the corporations makes no sense. Economic policy should not treat ecological considerations as peripheral. Ecological modernization is consistent with economic growth, and can sometimes be one of its motive forces.

(5)   Seeks to foster a diversified society based upon egalitarian principles. Social diversity is not compatible with a strongly defined egalitarianism of outcome. Third way politics looks instead to maximize equality of opportunity. However, this has to preserve a concern with limiting inequality of outcome too. The chief reason is that equality of opportunity can generate inequalities of wealth and income – that then hamper opportunities for subsequent generations.

Inequality can no longer, if it ever could, be countered only by income transfers from the more to the less affluent. Some forms of welfare provision, for example, designed in some part to reduce poverty, have had the effect of creating or perpetuating it. Moreover, the old 'project of exclusion' which drove social democracy – admitting the working class to full social, political and economic citizenship – has lapsed. Social democrats today need to combat newer forms of exclusion – at the bottom and at the top. At the bottom, 5% or so of the population risks becoming detached from the wider society – some, such as those imprisoned in decaying tower blocks, are casualties of the welfare state. At the top, an equivalent proportion, consisting mostly of affluent managers and professionals, may threaten to opt out of the wider society, into 'ghettos of the privileged'.

(6)   Takes globalization seriously. Many authors and

politicians, while recognizing the significance of globalization, concentrate only upon policies on a national plane. We must respond to global change on a local, national and world-wide level. Third way social democrats should look to transform existing global institutions and support the creation of new ones. The left in the past has always been internationalist. Socialists used to champion international solidarity and were the leaders in promoting the economic development of poorer countries – even if the strategies they endorsed were largely failures. Today, ironically, the old left has become isolationist, sometimes opposing almost every aspect of the global economy.[16] The intensifying of globalization, however – which in any case goes well beyond the economic marketplace alone – offers many benefits, which it should be the aim of third way politics to maximize.

In the rest of the book I shall try to develop each of the above points in greater detail, beginning with problems of state, government and economic policy.

[16] Alice H. Amsden and Takashi Hikino, 'The left and globalisation.' *Dissent* 46/2 (Spring, 1999): 7–9.

3

Government, the State and Economic Strategy

The third way, state and government

The traditional left, and many other social democrats too, tend to operate with an unreconstructed notion of the state. Their aim is to replace the market, as far as possible, with state power in order to realize social goals. Modernizing social democrats should argue for a different standpoint. In the wake of the receding influence of free-market philosophies, it is a fundamental task to revive public institutions. However, it won't do to identify public institutions solely with government and the state. Following the decline or collapse of the other 'ways', third way politics has to look for a different basis of social order.

Its point of view could be described as *structural pluralism*. The 'design options' offered by the two rival political positions were monistic – they looked either to government or to the market as the means of coordinating the social realm. Others have turned to the community or civil society as the ultimate sources of social cohesion. However, social order, democracy and social justice cannot be developed where one of these sets of institutions is dominant. A balance between them is required for a pluralistic society to be sustained. Moreover, each has to be looked at afresh in the light of contemporary social changes.

One of the lessons to be learned from the fall of communism, and from the statist zeal of old-style social democracy, is that – even when applied to desirable social ends – state power can become stifling and bureaucratic. The neoliberal opponents of big government, as Offe says, 'must be granted the point that excessive statism often inculcates dispositions of dependency, inactivity, rent-seeking, red tape, clientelism, authoritarianism, cynicism, fiscal irresponsibility, avoidance of accountability, lack of initiative, and hostility to innovation, if not outright corruption – and so often on either side of the administration–client divide'.[1]

These considerations explain the emphasis the third way places on personal responsibility, as well as upon the transparency and reform of state mechanisms. As against the traditional left, it is emphasized that it isn't only the market that creates perverse or disruptive consequences for those exposed to it. Government and the state do so as well and – just like the market – call forth active responses. Welfare clients, for instance, do not simply 'accept' benefits given to them. They react actively and with discrimination to what is on offer, while state

[1] Offe, 'The present historical transformation', p. 7.

action changes their social environments in unpredictable ways. In the example given earlier, provision for old age served to redefine what 'being old' actually is, and by no means only in a benign fashion.

Obviously social democrats should not join with the free-marketeers in denigrating the state and all its works. Government and the state perform many tasks essential to any civilized society. The democratic left believed in the mixed economy, and therefore saw the state and markets in some sort of balance. Yet there is no doubt that in many countries the state, national and local, became too large and cumbersome. The inefficiency and wastefulness that state institutions frequently display provided fertile ground for the growth of neoliberalism and diminished the standing of the public sphere as a whole. As private companies downsized, adopted flatter hierarchies and sought to become more responsive to customer needs, the limitations of bureaucratic state institutions stood out in relief.

Acknowledging these developments does not imply arguing that governments have to adopt a diminished role in the world. Reform of the state can give government more influence than before rather than less. There is a difference between a *big state*, as measured by the number of its functionaries or the size of its budget, and a *strong state*. In any given circumstance, we can ask: will a marginal increase in the scope of the state improve access of citizens to basic social and economic goods, or would a decrease actually serve these ends better?

The idea that the state should be reduced to a 'caretaker' capacity is plainly inadequate. The minimal state ideology ignores the limitations of markets just as thoroughly as the traditional left does the pathologies of the state. Government must play a basic role in sustaining the social and civic frameworks upon which markets actually depend. It is a fantasy, for example, to suppose that taxation can be reduced to a bare minimum and social order still be maintained, or economic prosperity created.

The reconstruction of public institutions, and confidence in their performance, is a first priority in contemporary societies. States have become inadequate in the provision of public goods, social protection, and civic order. The issue is not, as the critics seem to think, that the size of the state has fallen too far – on the contrary, in most societies it has stayed the same, or continued to grow. States can be simultaneously oversized *and* underperforming, and face legitimacy deficits as a result. But we need also to adjust government and state power to the exigencies of a globalizing era, with the changes in sovereignty this brings in its train. In addition, we have to address the requirements of governance that new risk situations bring about. These are mostly not 'traditional' demands, that can be met merely by providing further resources for existing state institutions.

Third way politics looks to transform government and the state – to make them as effective and quick on their feet as many sectors of business have now become. These aims have to be achieved through structural reform, not through turning state institutions into markets or quasi-markets. Many business firms have reformed themselves in recent years, but not by making themselves like markets. The most effective firms have debureaucratized, looked for the benchmarking of standards, and have accorded greater autonomy in decision-making to lower levels of the organization. Government should seek to achieve similar results within its own agencies.

It is quite untrue to say that the only way to breathe new life into public institutions is to privatize them, necessary though this sometimes may be. As an example, we can look at one such institution, the postal service in the country normally thought to be the home of privatized industry, the US. The US Post Service (USPS) had long been losing money – some $9 billion over two decades up to the mid-1990s. The USPS had become a byword for inefficiency, lampooned by comedians from coast to coast.[2] In New York State, for example, 92% of mail was supposed to be next-day delivery; the real rate in 1990 was only just over 50%. Many efforts had been made to restructure the service in the past, but all had foundered on the cumbersome nature of the gigantic bureaucracy involved. The USPS carries some 40% of the world's mail.

Yet in 1995 the service made one of the most remarkable turnarounds ever seen in any enterprise, moving from a loss of $800 million the previous year to a profit of $1.8 billion. Since then it has made substantial profits each year – the first time an increased profit had ever been made without postal price rises. The change was made by a thoroughgoing shake-up of the organization, designed to make every employee responsive to the needs of customers, with incentives for meeting stated aims.

[2] Simon Caulkin, 'Signed, sealed, delivered.' *Observer* (10 October 1999).

Those introducing the new system budgeted for a profit of $100 million in 1995 – and were taken aback by the fact that the real profit turned out to be eighteen times higher. By focusing upon the customer who pays the bills, the reforms provided quite a different orientation for the workforce, which had not previously had incentive opportunities. Bureaucratic rules of procedure were dissolved in favour of devolved decision-making, responsive to client needs. Next-day delivery targets are now nearly always met, or exceeded.

The self-reform of government and the state needs not only to meet efficiency goals, but to respond to the voter apathy from which even the most established democratic states are suffering. In many countries, levels of trust in political leaders and other authority figures have declined, while the proportions voting in elections and expressing an interest in parliamentary politics have also dropped.

A recent study compared the findings of opinion surveys in a number of industrial countries. In virtually all of them confidence in politicians is in decline. In Germany, for instance, the percentage of people who said they trusted their deputy in the Federal Parliament to represent their interests fell from 55% in 1978 to 34% in 1992. The proportion of Swedes who agreed with the statement that 'parties are only interested in people's votes, not their opinions', grew from 49% in 1968 to 72% in 1994. In 1996, only 19% of Swedish citizens expressed confidence in the national parliament.[3]

Interpreting such findings isn't easy. People might ex-

---

[3] 'Is there a crisis?', *The Economist* (17 July 1999).

pect more from the state than they used to, and thus feel disappointed with its performance. Rising standards of education, plus the easy availability of information, may make people more critical and sceptical than they once were. To some degree, ignoring what governments do can be a healthy feature of democracy. Yet in-depth research does indicate widespread disillusionment with orthodox parliamentary processes. The most systematic research on the issue has been carried out by Joseph Nye and his colleagues at the Kennedy School at Harvard University.[4] Many people feel that government has become remote from their everyday lives and concerns. They believe that politics has become a corrupt affair, distant from the democratic ideals that supposedly inspire it. Neither worry is easily remedied, since in an era of globalization national politicians have less control over some of the influences affecting their citizens than they did.

However, reform of government and the mechanisms of the state can contribute to redressing the balance. In what has become an open information society, the established democracies are *not democratic enough*. What is needed is a second wave of democratization – or what I call the democratizing of democracy.[5] The democratizing of democracy will require differing policies depending upon a country's history and its level of prior democratization. For many, it involves constitutional reform, the stripping away of archaic symbols and privileges, plus

---

[4] For a summary version, see Joseph Nye, 'In government we don't trust.' *Foreign Policy* 108 (Fall 1997): 99–111.
[5] Giddens, *The Third Way*, ch. 3.

measures to introduce greater transparency and accountability. It is also likely to include 'experiments with democratization' such as the use of electronic referenda,
revived forms of direct democracy and citizens' juries.

In a developing information order, the boundaries between what is acceptable political behaviour and what is
widely regarded as corrupt become altered. Old-boy networks, backstage deals, unashamed forms of patronage
– even in the most established democracies, these were
simply often 'the way things are done', accepted by those
in political circles and by the citizenry alike. They aren't
accepted as such any longer, at least by the wider population; and they have to be a principal target of the democratizing of democracy. It isn't by chance that new
calls for transparency are being made, not just of political institutions, but in other areas too. This is a logical
feature of a society in which access to information is far
easier than ever before and where secrecy is in retreat.

Second-wave democratization has to track the influence
of globalization. Hence it normally involves the devolution of power to localities and regions – but also the transfer
of democratic power upwards, above the level of the nation state. In Europe, the further democratizing of the
European Union is the most obvious vehicle whereby this
can be achieved. I discuss these possibilities in chapter 5.

Communitarianism and government

Disenchantment with neoliberal policies, plus the problems of governability just referred to, were factors lead-

ing to the rise of communitarian thinking over recent years. According to communitarians, the consolidating of communities, and of civil society as a whole, are to overcome the social disintegration brought about by the dominance of the marketplace. The communitarians have had a direct and visible influence upon the New Democrats and New Labour, as well as upon social democratic parties elsewhere. Communitarianism represents a 'call to restore civic virtues' and 'to shore up the moral foundations of society'.[6]

In the communitarian view, a stable sense of self has to be anchored in a community – such as one's family of origin, or ethnic, religious or national communities. Communities are the source of the ethical values that make a wholesome civic life possible. In a general way, such a view is surely correct. Moreover, contrary to what is sometimes assumed, globalization creates favourable conditions for the renewal of communities. This is because globalization has a 'push-down' effect, promoting the local devolution of power and bottom-up community activism.

Communitarianism, however, has its problems, well established in the now extensive literature to which it has given rise. The term 'community' does too much work in communitarian theory: a society or a nation, for example, is only a community in an elliptical sense. Moreover, if they become too strong, communities breed identity politics, and with it the potential for social divi-

---

[6] Amitai Etzioni, *The Spirit of Community*. London: Fontana, 1995, p. 31.

sion, or even disintegration. Even in its milder forms, identity politics tends to be exclusivist, and difficult to reconcile with the principles of tolerance and diversity upon which an effective civil society depends. Hence it is to civil society more generally, rather than to 'the community', that we should turn as an essential element of third way politics.

Civil society is fundamental to constraining the power of both markets and government. Neither a market economy nor a democratic state can function effectively without the civilizing influence of civic association. The neoliberal critics of big government imagine that freedom will be maximized by transferring power to the private sector. Yet as Benjamin Barber caustically observes,

> democracy is not a synonym for the marketplace, and the notion that by privatising government we can establish civil society and civic goods is a dishonourable myth. The freedom to buy a Coke or a Big Mac is not the freedom to determine how you will live and under what kind of regime . . . [the neoliberals make a] disastrous confusion between the moderate, mostly well-founded claim that flexibly regulated markets are the most efficient instruments of economic productivity and wealth accumulation, and the zany, overblown claim that unregulated markets are the sole means by which we can produce and distribute everything we care about . . .[7]

[7] Benjamin Barber, *A Place For Us*. New York: Hill & Wang, 1998, p. 72.

The state and government do not represent the public domain when they become detached from their roots in civic association. The rule of law, the basic prerequisite of democratic government, can't exist without unwritten codes of civic trust. Civil society, rather than the state, supplies the grounding of citizenship, and is hence crucial to sustaining an open public sphere.

Third way politics and economic globalization

In the reform of state and government, as well as in economic policy, third way politics looks to respond to the great social transformations of the end of the twentieth century: globalization, the rise of the new knowledge-based economy, changes in everyday life, and the emergence of an active, reflexive citizenry. Each of these refers to a complex of developments; moreover, each is connected with the others. The intensifying of globalization has been deeply influenced by the information technology revolution, while the knowledge economy itself is becoming globalized. At the same time, the rapid diffusion of information dissolves tradition and custom, enforcing a more active, open approach to life. Bound up as it also is with rapid scientific innovation, globalization contributes directly to the creation of new risks; it places a premium upon the effective management of both the dynamic and the threatening sides of risk-taking.

That economic globalization is real, and different from analogous processes in the past, has become increasingly difficult to dispute – whatever some of the critics might say.[8] This is most obviously true in the case of world currency markets. Average daily turnover on the global foreign exchange market has increased from $180 million twenty years ago to $1.5 trillion today. The total portfolio of cross-border holdings of bank deposits and loans grew from $1 billion in 1981 to $5.5 billion in 1996. These statistics represent more than just a very large increase in the volume of economic transactions. The basic character of the world economy has changed, partly because of the dominance of financial markets over trade in goods and commodities, and partly because of the ever-growing role of knowledge as a force of production.

The globalizing economy has a number of distinct features.[9] Science and technology, and human symbolic skills, play an increasingly essential role in productivity, and therefore in economic growth. Productivity in the advanced economies, unlike in earlier stages of capitalist development, is no longer so dependent upon the adding of capital or labour to the production process.

Information-processing activities are growing in im-

---

[8] For the best account of this debate see David Held, Anthony McGrew, David Goldblatt and Jonathan Perraton, *Global Transformations: Politics, Economics and Culture*. Cambridge: Polity Press, 1999.

[9] See Manuel Castells, 'The informational economy and the new international division of labor'. In Martin Carnoy, Manuel Castells, Stephen S. Cohen, and Fernando Henrique Cardoso, *The New Global Economy in the Information Age*. University Park, PA: Pennsylvania State University Press, 1993, pp. 15–43; Manuel Castells, *The Rise of the Network Society*. Cambridge, MA: Blackwell, 1996.

portance in terms of both their contribution to GDP and the proportion of the workforce involved. The increasing prominence of wired workers is more significant than the more general shift from manufacturing to services, because their activities quite often enter directly into production processes. A fundamental transition is taking place in the organization of production and of economic activity more generally – towards the creation of networks linking firms or parts of firms. Along with these, a growing role is played by small and medium-sized businesses in generating economic development. Even the giant corporations aren't protected from technological or market changes that can undermine their profitability almost overnight.

In the knowledge economy, there are increasingly permeable boundaries between industries or industrial sectors that used to be separate and distinct from one another. Thus banking and insurance can be done over the internet by companies bearing only a passing resemblance to those that have dominated these sectors; supermarkets sell domestic gas, while petrol stations double up as grocery stores and newsagents.

New forms of uncertainty are not only created by the global economy, they are intrinsic to achieving economic success.[10] Most of the key sources of growth just described are also sources of uncertainty, and anyone who wants to contribute to them must engage with it. The global availability of information adds to uncertainty rather than

[10] Michael J. Mandel, *The High-Risk Society*. New York: Times Business/Random House, 1996.

reducing it. For example, a corporate strategy that works won't give a company long-term security – it will rapidly be copied or outflanked.

As the uncertainties grow, so do the opportunities for innovation and profit, especially in technologically fast-moving areas of industry. Workers aren't exempt from these processes. Rewards might be considerable in high-tech companies, but since the pace of technological change is so rapid, jobs are likely to be very insecure. As the boundaries between key industries dissolve, the financial economy and the 'real' economy of goods and services come to share some common characteristics. Entry into a sector is easy, including for small competitors, relevant information is widely available for those who choose to seek it out, and profit opportunities are rapidly reacted to.

Globalization is by no means wholly economic in its nature, causes, or consequences.[11] It is a basic mistake to limit the concept to the global marketplace. Globalization is also social, political and cultural. On all of these levels, it is a highly uneven set of processes, proceeding in a fragmentary and oppositional fashion. While still dominated by the industrial nations, it isn't simply the same as Westernization – all countries in the world today are affected by globalization processes. Developments in science and technology, for example, affect people's lives in richer and poorer countries alike, and in a more immediate way than ever before.

[11] Anthony Giddens, *Runaway World*. London: Profile, 1999.

The knowledge economy

The knowledge economy is not as yet all-conquering, but it is well on the way to being so. In combination with the broader aspects of globalization, it marks a major transition in the nature of economic activity. Information technology, plus communications technology, are the enabling media of the new economy, but its agents are knowledge workers – wired workers and others whose work does not directly produce material goods. The know-how of such workers is the most valuable form of property that firms have. To assess the value of Microsoft, one wouldn't get far by asking about the factors conventionally used to assess value – land, plant, and raw materials. The tangible assets of the company are tiny compared to its market value. The market-to-book ratio of a company is the difference between its material assets and its saleable value. The market-to-book ratio of Microsoft is over 13. For General Motors, it is only 1.6.

The dynamic sectors of the economy today are in finance, computers and software, telecommunications, biotechnology and the communications industries. The telecommunications industry in the US employs more people than the car and car-parts industries combined. Measured in terms of annual turnover, the health and medical industry in the US is bigger than oil refining, aircraft and car production, logging, steel and shipping put together.

Industrial manufacture, of course, is still highly important, and to some extent has become redistributed to non-Western countries. However, most manufacturing processes have become closely integrated with information technology, as have retail and distribution. Moreover, ideas, image and brand name count for far more in generating profitability than efficiency of manufacture. Efficient manufacture is a bottom line, a necessary condition of profitability, but certainly not a sufficient one.

Societies or regions can move from an agrarian to a knowledge economy without passing through a phase of old-style industrialization. One example is the area around Chicago in the Great Lakes region, where agricultural markets were displaced by financial markets. The much-discussed 'Silicon Valley' of India in Bangalore is another illustration.

Since innovation and niche marketing are so important in the new economy, product cycles tend to be much faster than they once were. Car makers in Japan now work on a two-year cycle; Japanese manufacturers of electronics goods assume a cycle of three months. Financial markets move quickest of all. Some products have a life cycle of only a few hours – by then the competition has caught up.[12]

It has aptly been said that we have moved from a world where the big beat the small to a world where the fast beat the slow. In 1985 Intel released a new microprocessor, which worked far more effectively than its earlier chip. IBM at that time was telling its customers that if they bought its most up-to-date computer, it would guarantee the computer wouldn't be obsolete for five years.

[12] Don Tapscott, *The Digital Economy*. New York: McGraw-Hill, 1997.

Since IBM weren't interested in the Intel chip the company did a deal with Compaq. Compaq then took a massive section of IBM's business.

We are also moving from a world in which the heavy beat the light to one where the light beat the heavy.[13] The story of the *Encyclopaedia Britannica* makes the point tellingly. The *Encyclopaedia Britannica* was unrivalled as the world's best-selling encyclopaedia for two centuries. In the early 1990s, for the first time, it was overtaken – by two encyclopaedias published on CD-ROM, one of which was produced by Microsoft. The classic *Encyclopaedia Britannica* was a large, multi-volume work, fully updated once every ten years. The CD-based encyclopaedias had more content, cost less than a tenth of the book version, and were updated every three months.

The makers of the *Encyclopaedia Britannica* responded with a radical strategy. They put the whole of the work on the internet, and charged a daily fee for subscribers. In so doing, they outpaced the CD-ROMs: the content can be updated hourly, and much more information is available than is held on the CDs. The system has 'hot links' that allow subscribers to connect to web servers, making all the information on the web a resource. *Britannica* became a subscription and licensing service, having agreements with many educational institutions. In October 1999 it was announced that *Britannica* would be offered free on the net – all 44 million words of it. The

---

[13] Thomas L. Friedman, *The Lexus and the Olive Tree*. New York: Farrar, 1999.

71

company plans to recoup the expense by means of e-commerce and advertising revenues. But will it last in this new guise for another 200 years? It seems exceedingly unlikely.

Government will not be able to play an effective role in the new economy if it goes on the defensive. As the transformations noted above occur, citizens will need the help of government just as much as they used to; but state intervention has to be redirected, and cooperation with other agencies will be essential.

We could think of the influences involved as a triangle:

Finance

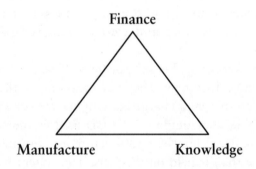

Manufacture   **Knowledge**

In the old economy, industrial manufacture was the dominant point of the triangle. Financial markets were geared to the needs of industrial production, although of course they always had a life of their own. In the globalizing economy, financial markets have much more autonomy – in effect, they scrutinize the efforts of producers. Knowledge is much less subservient to manufacture, since it becomes more and more the key to productivity. Financial markets grow increasingly diverse, driven as they are by the increasing complexity of available market knowledge. Control of manufacturing capital, the regulation of financial markets – these remain major tasks for left-of-centre governments. But the other point of the triangle becomes even more important. Government needs to build a 'knowledge base' that will release the full potential of the information economy.

Old-style social democracy concentrated on industrial policy and Keynesian demand measures, while the neoliberals focused on deregulation and market liberalization. Third way economic policy needs to concern itself with different priorities – with education, incentives, entrepreneurial culture, flexibility, devolution and the cultivation of social capital. Third way thinking emphasizes that a strong economy presumes a strong society, but doesn't see this connection as coming from old-style interventionism. The aim of macroeconomic policy is to keep inflation low, limit government borrowing, and use active supply-side measures to foster growth and high levels of employment.

The key force in human capital development obviously has to be education. It is the main public investment that can foster both economic efficiency and civic cohesion. Education isn't a static input into the knowledge economy, but is itself becoming transformed by it. It has traditionally been seen as a preparation for life – an attitude that persisted as it became more and more widely available. Primary school education became mandatory for everyone, then an extended period of secondary school education. Higher education expanded, taking on increasing numbers of students. But the underlying idea remained that of acquiring the qualifications needed to get a start in adulthood.

Education needs to be redefined to focus on capabilities that individuals will be able to develop through life. Orthodox schools and other educational institutions are likely to be surrounded, and to some extent subverted, by a diversity of other learning frameworks. Internet technology, for instance, might bring educational opportunities to mass audiences. In the old economic order, the basic competencies needed for jobs remained relatively constant. Learning (and forgetting – being able to discard old habits) are integral to work in the knowledge economy. A worker creating a novel multimedia application can't succeed by using long-standing skills – the tasks in question didn't even exist a short while ago.

Policies that protect uncompetitive industries, or select 'national champions', can at most have a transitional use. Government investments in a troubled industry may help tide it over while adjustments or innovations are made, but more far-reaching interventions can be counter-productive or even disastrous. If IBM had been chosen as a national champion, and protected by government in the 1980s, its rising competitors, such as Apple, Microsoft and Intel, would probably have been frozen out. The US, at least for the time being, now has a position of leadership in these industries.

Government can take some supply-side initiatives relevant to these developments, as the US government did in respect of information technology. Investment in relevant areas of science and technology is one significant

factor. Another is helping create the conditions that encourage entrepreneurship – a phenomenon that again
concerns not only private industry, but the state and civil
society too.

Entrepreneurs have received short shrift from both the
old left and the neoliberals.[14] The left has seen entrepreneurs as selfishly profit-driven, concerned to extract as
much surplus value as possible from the labour force.
Neoliberal theory stresses the rationality of competitive
markets, where decision-making is driven by market
needs. Successful entrepreneurs, however, are innovators,
because they spot possibilities that others miss, or take
on risks that others decline, or both. A society that doesn't
encourage entrepreneurial culture won't generate the economic energy that comes from the most creative ideas.
Social and civic entrepreneurs are just as important as
those working directly in a market context, since the same
drive and creativity are needed in the public sector, and
in civil society, as in the economic sphere.

The question of flexibility

Product, capital and labour markets must all be flexible
for an economy today to be competitive. 'Flexibility' for
many is a red rag to a bull. Especially as applied to labour markets, flexibility implies deregulation, making
workers more vulnerable to economic insecurity and ex-

[14] Charles Leadbeater, *Living on Thin Air: The New Economy*. London: Viking, 1999.

panding the numbers of in-work poor. Flexibility does indeed entail deregulation – getting rid of, or reshaping, rules and regulations that hamper innovation and technological change. Increasing flexibility can't be costless – trade-offs are involved. Yet it can't be stressed too strongly how high the social and personal costs are where there is large-scale unemployment, and especially where there are many long-term unemployed.

The statistics on job creation are instructive. In almost all industrial countries there are more jobs now than a quarter of a century ago. The sole exceptions are Sweden, Finland, and Spain. In the US 45% more net jobs were created over that period and in Canada almost as many. For Japan, the figure is 24%. In the EU countries, on the other hand, there was on average only a 4% growth in jobs. A high proportion – about half – of the new net jobs created in the US were in skilled or professional occupations. Contrary to some interpretations, those who have profited most, in relative terms, are women and ethnic minority groups, including Afro-Americans.

Among the twenty-five largest US companies today, all save six were either very small or didn't exist before 1960. The story in Europe is quite different. All the twenty-five biggest firms were in existence at that date. The problem in Europe is that innovative small firms don't grow into big ones. In some countries, firms actually fight to stay small, since they avoid government rules and regulations. In northern Italy there are many successful small firms. They stay at a size of under 1,000 workers because this keeps them outside the rules that otherwise come into play. The same happens in Germany. Firms with less than 2,000 employees don't have to conform with the laws on co-determination. Some companies downsize and subcontract out everything they can in order to stay below that level.

So far as labour markets go, two competing perspectives are involved in European politics at the moment. The French Socialist Party is attempting different solutions from those suggested elsewhere, such as the UK, Holland or Denmark. The Socialists propose to create 700,000 minimum-wage jobs, largely financed by government, half in the state sector and half in private industry. By early 1999 some 100,000 jobs had been identified and filled, all of them in the state and voluntary sectors. A second element of the party's strategy is the thirty-five-hour working week, scheduled to be introduced in January 2000 in firms with more than twenty workers.

A statutory thirty-five-hour working week would seem to be the opposite of flexibility, but there are some signs that it is in fact helping to promote it. French employers are seeking to introduce shift working and weekend working, coupled with more part-time working, as means of adapting fruitfully to the directive. If these changes occur, the initiative could bear fruit. On the other hand, if it is applied rigidly, it is likely to block needed reforms rather than obviate the need for them.

Some leftist critics say that active labour market policies are essentially irrelevant, because the jobs have to be there in the first place. The most important mechanism of job creation is economic growth. But economic growth does not solve labour market problems on its own. Thus between 1984 and 1994 the EU countries had average growth rates of 2.3%, in spite of the negligible increase in the net number of new jobs.

Whether labour market flexibility inevitably increases the numbers of working poor is a question I shall consider in the next chapter.

Social capital

The cultivation of social capital is integral to the knowledge economy. The 'new individualism' that goes along with globalization is not refractory to cooperation and collaboration -- cooperation (rather than hierarchy) is positively stimulated by it. Social capital refers to trust networks that individuals can draw upon for social support, just as financial capital can be drawn upon to be used for investment. Like financial capital, social capital can be expanded – invested and reinvested.

Since the time at which it was first popularized by the sociologist James Coleman, the idea of social capital has been so widely deployed that some think it has been drained of much of its value. Yet its usefulness resides in the wide application it can have. It is of prime importance in civil society – it makes possible the everyday civility that is crucial to effective public life. In the context of the new economy, it has a more specific significance. It is the basis of the networks that play a major role in innovation. Coordination costs are lowered through shared norms rather than through bureaucratic hierarchy.

Some years ago, the concept of social capital was widely employed to show why 'Rhineland capitalism', together with the Japanese and the East Asian economies, were superior to other forms. In these societies, it was argued, dense trust networks provided a platform for stable and successful economic growth.

The argument wasn't completely wrong, but it ignored two core limitations of these trust systems. Trust shaded over too easily into cronyism and even corruption. Moreover, trust wasn't primarily 'active trust' – it was based upon established routines, in relatively inflexible institutions, instead of being open and actively negotiated. Rather different trust relationships have been involved in industries at the forefront of the knowledge economy. Take as an example the biotechnology industry in the US. In that industry, there is a great deal of formal collaboration among firms, universities and research laboratories. Over 80% of firms in human therapeutics and diagnostics have formal ties with other biotech firms, as well as a variety of more informal types of collaboration. Research studies have shown that nearly all successful biotech companies are highly active collaborators. None of the isolated firms covered in these studies were successful.[15] Such trust relationships generate innovation precisely because they are fluid and diverse.

Innovation in the old economy was often the result of separate processes of research, development and production. In the knowledge-based economy, innovation stems more from networks and collaborative ventures. Firms

---

[15] Jane E. Fountain, 'Social capital: a key enabler of innovation.' In *Investing in Innovation*, ed. L. M. Branscomb and J. H. Keller. Cambridge, MA: MIT Press, 1998.

are increasingly turning to networks of suppliers and customers to develop novel ideas and technologies. There were only 750 inter-firm alliances registered in the US during the 1970s. Between 1987 and 1992 there were 20,000. The range of industry ties with universities has also grown rapidly.

The spread of information technology itself is one factor promoting these collaborations, since the same base of technology can be drawn upon by different specialists. For instance, the pen maker A. T. Cross developed the hardware for its digital notepad, while IBM developed the software. Industry–research collaborations have also grown as a means of pooling investment and risk.

Recognition of the importance of ongoing networks of learning and innovation has proceeded further in the private sector than in government in most countries. Governments should be looking for policies that enhance alliances, save where these lead to monopoly – not a problem with the small and medium-sized firms which are mostly the leaders. A number of possible policy avenues exist. Tax credits can be given for industry investments in research groups, or for partnerships between industry and research institutions. Challenge grants can be provided for innovation partnerships between small or medium-sized firms and universities or other comparable institutions.

The US, or certain economic sectors of it, is usually quoted as the main example of the connections between active social capital, innovation and productivity. But other countries offer equally fertile ground for it, and suggest a larger role for government. An example is provided by Denmark. The Danish economy is dominated by small and medium-sized businesses, mixing the hard edge of competition with networks of interdependence. Policy-makers in government and industry have sought to strengthen collaboration between firms as a means of enhancing overall economic competitiveness. A series of initiatives has been introduced, such as the 'network programme' set up in 1989. The aim was to encourage binding collaboration between networks of at least three firms, with 'network brokers', who were to identify and support cooperative ventures. Follow-up research indicates the programme was successful, in terms of directly economic criteria as well as the range and density of collaborations established. When a social democrat-led coalition government came to power in 1993–4, these early endeavours were followed by a much more encompassing policy following similar lines. Government intervention concentrates upon the 'framework conditions' of economic development and competitiveness, not upon direct subsidies of any kind.[16]

In the past, some on the left have viewed the 'third sector' (the voluntary sector) with suspicion. Government and other professional agencies should as far as possible take over from third-sector groups, which are often amateurish and dependent upon erratic charitable impulses. Developed in an effective manner, however, third-sector groups can offer choice and responsiveness in the delivery of public services. They can also help promote local

[16] Ash Amin and Damian Thomas, 'The negotiated economy: state and civic institutions in Denmark.' *Economy and Society* 25/2 (1996): 255–81.

civic culture and forms of community development. To do so they need to be active and entrepreneurial. Social entrepreneurs can be highly effective innovators in the realm of civil society, at the same time contributing to economic development. They can

> operate as a kind of research and development wing of the welfare system, innovating new solutions to intractable social problems. They often deliver services far more efficiently than the public sector. Most importantly they set in motion a virtuous circle of social capital accumulation. They help communities to build up social capital which gives them a better chance of standing on their own two feet.[17]

Third-sector groups can also combine effectively with business to foster social programmes. Rosabeth Moss Kanter's work, based on comparative research carried out in different cities and regions of the US, is instructive in this respect. She found a number of companies, and groups of companies, becoming involved in social development in ways quite different from the past. Businesses have usually supported the social sector either by giving money to community activities or by contributing their employees' time for volunteer work. They have treated the third sector as a 'dumping ground' for 'spare cash, obsolete equipment and tired executives on their way out'. [18] Such

[17] Charles Leadbeater, *The Rise of the Social Entrepreneur*. London: Demos, 1997, pp. 9–10.
[18] Rosabeth Moss Kanter, 'From spare change to real change: the social sector as a site for business innovation.' *Harvard Business Review* 77/3 (May–June 1999): 122–32, 128.

philanthropy at arm's length has made little dent upon America's enduring social problems. The 'new paradigm', as Moss Kanter calls it, is quite different. It involves using social needs as a basis for the development of ideas, technologies and long-term investments. The firms concerned are using their best people and cutting-edge technologies.

An example is the programme begun by Bell Atlantic in the early 1990s, installing computer networks in schools. The company gave state-of-the-art computers to students to use at home, allowing them access to the network for interactive learning activities. Most of the students were from poor backgrounds, while the schools concerned were close to failing. The schools have since become national role models, while the company gained from the experience by discovering new ways of handling data transmission in the service of education.

Sceptical observers, Moss Kanter points out, are liable to see such endeavours simply as 'public relations ploys'. But, in the cases she studied, 'this would be an extremely costly and risky way to get a favourable press'. The primary justification 'is the new knowledge and capabilities that will stem from innovation'.

Conclusion

Reform of government and the state, a core theme of third way politics, is closely related to the economic changes signalled by the knowledge economy. In the contemporary world, contrary to what the neoliberals say, we need more government than before, not less. However, such government has to track the impact of globalization, and must stretch both below and above the level of the nation state. In an increasingly fast-moving world, government and the state also need to be quick on their feet, as well as democratic and transparent.

The economic interventions of government have to be different from those of the past. Those on the old left always say 'regulate, regulate', and greater regulation of economic life, in some respects and some contexts, is necessary. But deregulation can also be just as important, in areas where restrictions inhibit innovation, job creation or other basic economic goals. Government is not there only to constrain markets and technological change – it has just as significant a role in helping them work for the social good. To do so, it will often have to draw upon the resources of civil society; these resources are needed for effective governance too. All these considerations are also relevant to the issue of inequality, to which I now turn.

4

The Question of Inequality

Social democrats must revise not only their approach to, but also their concept of, equality in the wake of the decline of socialism. On the face of things, nothing would seem more obvious, yet many on the more traditional left seem to accept this only grudgingly. There is no future for the 'egalitarianism at all costs' that absorbed leftists for so long. Michael Walzer has put the point very well:

> Simple equality of that sort is the bad utopianism of the old left . . . political conflict and the competition for leadership always make for power inequalities and entrepreneurial activity always makes for economic inequalities . . . None of this can be prevented without endless tyrannical interventions in ordinary life. It was an historical mistake of large proportions, for which we [on the left] have paid heavily. . . .[1]

---

[1] M. Walzer, 'Pluralism and social democracy.' *Dissent* (Winter 1998): 47–53, 50.

The contemporary left needs to develop a dynamic, life-chances approach to equality, placing the prime stress upon equality of opportunity. Modernizing social democrats also have to find an approach that reconciles equality with pluralism and lifestyle diversity, recognizing that the clashes between freedom and equality to which classical liberals have always pointed are real. Equality of opportunity, of course, has long been a theme of the left and has been widely enshrined in policy, especially in the field of education. Yet many on the left have found it difficult to accept its correlates – that incentives are necessary to encourage those of talent to progress and that equality of opportunity typically creates higher rather than lower inequalities of outcome. Equality of opportunity also tends to produce high levels of social and cultural diversity, since individuals and groups have the chance to develop their lives as they see fit.

Rather than seeking to suppress these consequences we should accept them. Social democrats should be happy to acknowledge that this position brings them closer to ethical liberalism than many used to think. Alan Ryan is right to point to the affinities between third way politics and the ideas of the ethical liberals.

T. H. Green, Leonard Hobhouse, and others who thought like them distanced themselves from socialism and took an affirmative attitude towards market mechanisms. Economic competition is desirable, Hobhouse argued, but it presumes community and cooperation, which must have an ethical base. Government and the state shouldn't 'feed, house, or clothe' its citizens, but should 'secure conditions upon which its citizens are able to win by their own efforts all that is necessary to a full civic efficiency'.[2] There are reciprocal obligations, Hobhouse emphasized, between the individual and government; public and private concerns have to be in balance.

The ethical liberals insisted that the state should not undermine personal autonomy. Arnold Toynbee stressed that voluntary organizations – such as Toynbee Hall – should be developed so as to cultivate people's personal capabilities. Education, understood in a broad sense rather than purely vocationally, was to be the main instrument in cultivating initiative and responsibility.

These ideas have a clear affinity with some of the themes of contemporary third way politics. Yet the third way isn't, and can't be, just a reversion to ethical liberalism. The ethical liberals wrote before, or during, the rise of socialism as a major political force, whereas we are living after its demise. We have to construct policies of social justice that respond to the causes of that demise, which have created quite different exigencies from those of the past.

Here more recent authors are more instructive than the ethical liberals. Amartya Sen's concept of 'social capability' makes an appropriate starting-point.[3] Equality and inequality don't just refer to the availability of social and material goods – individuals must have the capability to make effective use of them. Policies designed to

[2] L. T. Hobhouse, *Liberalism*. London: Williams & Norgate, 1911, pp. 148 and 152.
[3] Amartya Sen, *Inequality Reexamined*. Oxford: Clarendon Press, 1992.

promote equality should be focused upon what Sen calls the 'capability set' – the overall freedom a person has to pursue his or her well-being. Disadvantage should similarly be defined as 'capability failure' – not only loss of resources, but loss of freedom to achieve.

Freedom defined as social capability isn't close to the self-seeking agent presumed in neoliberal economic theory. Individuals, as the communitarians say, exercise freedom precisely through their membership of groups, communities and cultures. It is not only individual choice that is at the core of pluralism, but also the diversity of cultures and groups to which individuals belong.

Equality and inequality revolve around self-realization. Apart from where people lack even the minimal requirements for physical survival, the same is true of poverty. What matters isn't economic deprivation as such, but the consequences of such deprivation for individuals' well-being. People who choose to live frugally are in quite a different position from those whose existence is blighted by unwanted poverty. A similar principle applies in terms of the life cycle. A person who is temporarily impoverished, but who, for whatever reason, is able to break free from poverty, is in a different situation from those mired in poverty in the long term.

A further example is unemployment. An individual who is unemployed might be living in a society that pays high levels of social security. Although economically in the same position as someone in work, or close to it, that person might be worse off in terms of well-being, because enforced unemployment is widely associated with lack of self-esteem and with the 'oppression of surplus time'.

The Question of Inequality

An emphasis on equality of opportunity, it should be
made clear, still presumes redistribution of wealth and
income. There are several reasons why, but two are worth
mentioning in particular.[4] One is that since equality of
opportunity produces inequality of outcome, redistribution is necessary because life-chances must be reallocated
across the generations. Without such redistribution, 'one
generation's inequality of outcome is the next generation's inequality of opportunity'.[5] A second is that there
will always be people for whom opportunities will ne-
cessarily be limited, or who are left behind when others
do well. They should not be denied the chance to lead
fulfilling lives.

With these various points in mind, we can move to look
briefly at the basic statistics of inequality in contemporary societies.

Comparing inequalities

It is generally accepted that inequalities of income and
wealth declined in most industrial countries over the
period from 1950 to 1970. Since the early 1970s they
have risen again in the majority of developed societies,
although not in all. As measured by the official statistics
at least, the developed countries differ considerably in
terms of inequality. Those having the highest levels of

[4] Giddens, *The Third Way*, pp. 101–4.
[5] James Tobin, 'A liberal agenda.' In *The New Inequality*, ed. Richard B. Freeman. Boston: Beacon, 1999, pp. 58–61.

income equality include the Nordic countries, Belgium and Japan. In the middle are societies such as the UK, France, the Netherlands and Germany. Countries with the highest degree of income inequality, as measured by official statistics, are the US, Israel, Italy and Australia.

The US appears as the most unequal of all industrial countries in terms of income distribution. The proportion of income taken by the top 1% has increased substantially over the past two or three decades, while those at the bottom have seen their average incomes stagnate or decline. Defined as 50% or less of median income, poverty in the US in the early 1990s was five times as great as in Norway or Sweden – 20% for the US, as compared to 4% for the other two countries. The incidence of poverty in Canada and Australia is also high, at 14% and 13% respectively.

Although the average level of income inequality in the European Union countries is lower than in the US, poverty is widespread in the EU according to official figures and measures. Using the criterion of half or less of median income, 57 million people were living in poverty in the EU nations in 1998. About two-thirds of these were in the largest societies: France, Italy, the UK and Germany.

Economic inequality, by and large, has been on the increase, but it would be misleading just to say bluntly, as some do, that the industrial countries have become more unequal than they once were. In some countries – Italy is one example – inequality has gone down, as measured by the usual statistics. Moreover, since 1996 the trend towards increasing income inequality in the US has been reversed. The numbers living below the poverty line have also dropped. In 1998 there were nearly 5 million fewer people in poverty than in 1992. The incomes of blacks and Hispanics in the US rose by 15% over that period.

There are other changes that run counter to increasing inequality. For example, in economic as well as social and cultural terms women have become much more equal to men than they used to be. 'Social egalitarianism', as measured in opinion surveys, has also increased. As one observer puts it: 'In my perception, people now care more rather than less about equality. They are more insistent on their standing as equals (what makes him think he is better than I? What makes her think she can tell me what to do?), less prepared to accept a subordinate position or believe everything the authorities say.'[6] In most industrial countries socially stigmatized groups, such as gays, or the disabled, have made progress towards full social acceptance.

The consequences of such changes are complex. The fact that children and women are now over-represented among the poor, for instance, partly reflects the wider gains that women as a whole have made. There are more single mothers than before, and single mothers on average have lower incomes than their married or coupled counterparts. At least one of the reasons for the rise in numbers of single-parent households is the increasing autonomy of women. Women actively leave unsatisfactory marriages more of-

[6] Anne Phillips, *Which Equalities Matter?* Cambridge: Polity Press, 1999, pp. 130–1.

ten than they were able to do before; and the number of never-married women with children has climbed.

The orthodox statistics about inequality and poverty are collected in the aggregate from year to year, and provide no data on shifts in individuals' economic circumstances across the life cycle. Until recently, we simply didn't know much about such shifts. Most approaches have assumed that poverty is a long-term condition. Even researches involving in-depth studies of individuals have nearly all been concerned with movement into poverty, rather than out of it. Only those currently in poverty are usually interviewed or studied. In addition, a good deal of research has concentrated upon groups unrepresentative of the poor as a whole, such as people living in inner-city ghetto areas – where poverty is often of long duration.

Recent research has suggested we should alter our way of thinking about poverty and the policies aimed at reducing it. Data from a number of countries show that, for the majority who experience it, poverty is not a permanent condition demanding long-term social assistance programmes. A surprising number of people escape from poverty – but a greater number than used to be thought also experience poverty at some point in their lives. Using the definition of 50% or under of median equivalent income, researchers in Germany found that over 30% of West Germans were poor for at least one year between 1984 and 1994. This figure is three times the maximum number of poor in any one year.[7] Those who moved out

---

[7] Lutz Leisering and Stephan Leibfried, *Time and Poverty in Western Welfare States*. Cambridge: Cambridge University Press, 1999.

of poverty mostly did not become stuck just above the poverty line. They reached a level of two-thirds of the national average when they were not poor. However, more than half returned to poverty during at least one year over the ten-year period.

A study carried out in the UK interviewed a national sample of adults each year from 1991 to 1996, to investigate shifts in income. The researchers found a great deal of income mobility, most of it short-range. Just over a third became poor for at least one year over the period.[8] 'Time is not simply the medium in which poverty occurs', one contributor observes, 'it forges its very nature.'[9] Research carried out by the Organization for Economic Cooperation and Development compared the US, UK, Germany and Canada.[10] The results showed that 20–40% of the population were in poverty for at least one year over a six-year period. Most were poor only for short spells. 2–6% remained poor over the whole period. However, because of their long stay in poverty, they made up fully a third of the total time all individuals spent below the poverty line. Contrary to the 'static statistics', the research showed that a higher percentage of people experienced poverty in Germany than in the other countries.

Disentangling the causes of increasing economic in-

[8] Stephen P. Jenkins, 'Income dynamics in Britain, 1991–6.' In *Persistent Poverty and Lifetime Inequality*, ed. John Hills. London: CASE, 1999, pp. 3–8.
[9] Robert Walker, 'Lifetime poverty dynamics.' In *Persistent Poverty and Lifetime Inequality*, ed. Hills, pp. 9–16.
[10] Howard Oxley: 'Poverty dynamics in four OECD countries.' In *Persistent Poverty and Lifetime Inequality*, ed. Hills, pp. 22–7.

equality is not easy. Only a few studies have investigated the issue in a detailed and systematic way, most of them coming from the United States. The results, however, are interesting and important. According to such research, in spite of the forcefulness with which the argument is sometimes pressed, free trade seems the least important influence. Skilled workers in the industrial countries are supposedly at an increasing disadvantage when compared to their counterparts elsewhere, who will work for much lower wages. Hence wages are driven down in the developed economies, and job opportunities become fewer. However, disparities of income have not grown only, or even primarily, in industries where trade is important, suggesting other factors are at work. Moreover, if the thesis were correct, the share of world commodity trade held by the industrial countries should have declined significantly over the past two decades. In fact, this hasn't happened. The proportion taken by the most developed countries has grown rather than shrunk. Ireland, Portugal and Austria, among others, have greatly increased their share. Even those which have lost out in relative terms, such as the UK, Sweden, or France, are exporting as much as they did twenty years ago.

The same applies to industrial output. The proportion held by the affluent countries, at 80%, has declined only slightly since 1980. Over this period, production for the world as a whole has doubled, while the Asian countries, particularly China, have vastly increased their output. Since the world economy as a whole has expanded, the continued share held by the industrial countries has proved compatible with increased production elsewhere.

The Question of Inequality

The East Asian successes have not happened at the expense of Western industrial workers. The West exports more to them than they do in return, as is true of the relation between Western manufacture and Third World countries as a whole.

Technological change is more important than global free trade. The spread of information technology leads to a declining demand for unqualified workers, whose job opportunities and wages therefore also decline. At the same time, those with skills or a strong educational background are able to increase their productivity and their earning power, pulling further away. One of the most in-depth studies we have suggests that technological change also accounts for part, but only part, of the increased income inequality observable in the US over the period 1990–6.[11] Most of that increase, the research concludes, is due to the other factors – demographic trends, changing work patterns in families and growing inequalities coming from non-labour sources, particularly capital assets. Less than 30% of the overall rise in inequality in the US between 1969 and 1992 is accounted for by earnings inequality among men in work. There are increasingly affluent members of two-earner families plus childless people who are economically successful. Houses, shares and pension funds, rising in value over the period, have added to their prosperity.

---

[11] Gary Burtless, 'Technological change and international trade: how well do they explain the rise in US income inequality?' In *The Inequality Paradox*, ed. James A. Auerbach and Richard S. Belous. Washington: National Policy Association, 1998, p. 29.

The Question of Inequality

Taxation and redistribution

Social democracy traditionally has a straightforward and morally compelling solution to inequality: take from the rich and give to the poor. Can such a formula still be applied today? The answer is that it can and should be. Modernizing social democrats should accept the core importance of progressive taxation as a means of economic redistribution.

Taking from the rich to give to the poor, however, isn't the simple and sovereign solution it seems to be on the surface. A diversity of problems has to be confronted.

(1)   We first have to decide who 'the rich' are. In the case of Bill Gates and other billionaires this doesn't cause too many difficulties. So far as income tax is concerned, however, the category of 'the rich' has to include large numbers of the merely affluent if it is to generate significant revenue and have a substantial redistributive effect. We also have to consider the factor of upward mobility. Bill Gates made his money from nothing. The possibility of becoming very wealthy is presumably not something that should be denied to people, since it may motivate exceptional talent. Moreover, even taking a good deal of Gates's wealth away from him wouldn't help others very much. The extent of his earnings partly reflects the greatly enlarged size of modern economies. A magnate like J. P. Morgan held a level of wealth that meant something in the US economy. At one point he had sufficient liquid capital to finance all the capital needs in America for four months. He owned less than a third of

the assets Bill Gates has. Yet Bill Gates's money could finance the current American economy for only part of a single day.

(2)   It is no longer feasible, or desirable, to have very steeply graduated income tax of the sort that existed in many countries up to thirty or so years ago. All countries have pulled back from such a practice, although some have done so more radically than others. To some extent, this change has been enforced – the better-off sections of the electorate have become resistant to paying very high tax rates. High rates of income tax hence increase levels of tax evasion, a phenomenon pointed to in the celebrated Laffer curve. Lowering taxes in some contexts can lead to an increase in tax revenue. One certainly cannot assume that higher tax rates always result in higher tax revenues. A luxury tax on boats introduced in 1991 in the US resulted in a dramatic fall in revenues as the entire luxury boat industry nearly disappeared. Just as important as these considerations is the fact that steeply graduated income tax can act as a disincentive, penalizing effort and therefore job creation and economic prosperity.

(3)   Social democrats should therefore rid themselves of the idea that most social problems can be resolved through increasing taxes to the greatest extent possible. In some situations the reverse theorem applies – tax cuts can both make economic sense and contribute to social justice. If carefully applied, tax cuts can increase supply-side investment, creating more profit and more disposable income. A bigger tax base is thereby created in the economy as a whole. Other tax-cutting

strategies, such as the Earned Income Tax Credit pioneered by the New Democrats in the US, can also be brought into play.

(4) Fiscal policy has become inseparable from processes of reform of government and the state. Governments can no longer 'take' taxes from their citizens without ensuring that the revenue is spent effectively, in a framework of transparency. Research shows that in most EU countries as well as in the US, a majority of the population feels that the government 'wastes a great deal of taxpayers' money'. This is one of the reasons many give for being prepared to engage in tax evasion. In a survey in Germany, 70% said they would consider 'a major violation' of the tax laws if the opportunity was there, on the grounds that the government squanders the revenues it derives from taxation.[12]

(5) We have to decide exactly how best to help the poor and the less privileged. There is a general relation between economic equality and levels of spending on the welfare state. The Scandinavian countries, which spend more than most others, are the most egalitarian. Yet it does not follow that spending more on existing welfare systems will help to alleviate inequality. The Scandinavian welfare state has its own specific difficulties. As Gøsta Esping-Andersen says of Sweden, 'from left to right, most analysts of the Swedish model now concur that the extremely egalitarian wage structure gives disincentives to work additional hours, or to augment skills and educa-

---

[12] Bodo Hombach, *A New Awakening: The Politics of the New Centre in Germany*. Cambridge: Polity Press, 2000.

tion. The marginal wage gain is simply too low.'[13] Sweden does not do well in international statistics in terms of its average levels of schooling and educational attainment. As mentioned earlier, it is also one of the very few Western countries to have suffered an absolute decline in terms of net jobs created over the past twenty years.

Assessing and comparing different taxation systems, especially in terms of their redistributive effects, is a complex task. Some general conclusions relevant to policy, however, can be drawn. Comparison of Western countries shows that in all of them the tax and transfer system does have redistributive effects. Sweden stands at the top: its tax and transfer system reduces inequality by 50% from market income to disposable net income. The US is lowest, with a reduction of 20%. The UK and Australia have reductions of around 25%, Finland 30%, Denmark and Germany 40%.

Taxes and transfers combine in various permutations to produce these consequences. One study looked at two aspects of income tax in this respect – level of taxation and progressiveness.[14] For example, the Australian income tax system in the mid-1980s was steeply progressive, but had relatively low overall levels of taxation. The Swedish tax system, by contrast, had considerably higher taxation levels, but a low degree of progressiveness. Much

[13] Gøsta Esping-Andersen, *The Three Worlds of Welfare Capitalism.* Cambridge: Polity Press, 1990.
[14] Rune Ervik, 'The Redistributive Aim of Social Policy.' Syracuse: Maxwell School of Citizenship and Public Policy, 1998.

the same was true of Denmark. The Nordic welfare states, together with Germany, have a more universal social transfer system, with high benefit levels. The researchers concluded that levels of taxation, coupled to social transfers, are more important sources of redistribution than the degree of progressiveness of income tax. The Nordic welfare states create a significant transfer of income to households with low market incomes, but also to those with higher incomes too. Australia and the UK are the only two countries where the income tax system is more important than the social transfer system in reducing economic inequality.

The implications of all this are fairly clear, although not easy to implement. Social democrats in all countries need to sustain a substantial tax base, if public and welfare policies are to be funded and economic inequality kept under control. They need to do so in the context of the reform and further democratization of the state itself. Progressive income tax needs to play a role in reducing inequalities, but it is neither sensible nor necessary to try to return to the steeply progressive systems of the past. In general, social democrats should continue to move away from heavy reliance on taxes that might inhibit effort or enterprise, including income and corporate taxes. Seeking to build up the tax base through policies designed to maximize employment possibilities is a sensible approach – indeed, it is a key emphasis of third way politics.

Obviously taxes that discourage the production of 'bads', most notably green taxes, should be relied upon as much as is feasible. It is not clear as yet how much income can be raised through eco-taxation, but the possibilities seem considerable. Shifting taxation onto energy, waste and transport, and away from labour or environmentally friendly business activities can be achieved in a number of ways. Terry Barker simulated a number of ecological reform packages for the British economy. For instance, carbon/energy taxes could be increased over a five-year period. The extra revenue generated would be used to reduce employers' national insurance contributions, and fund a domestic energy-saving programme to protect the poor. The projected results were compared with a scenario in which the economy carried on as before. Over a ten-year period, the changes would generate 0.1% more economic growth and create 278,000 extra jobs.[15]

In general, moving taxation towards consumption, as virtually all the industrial countries have done, makes political and economic sense. If consumption were taxed progressively, rather than only income, the incentive to save would be higher. Saving and investment are major engines of longer-term economic growth. Collecting such taxes need not be more complicated than collecting income tax. Receipts wouldn't have to be kept for every purchase; taxable value could be calculated on the difference between current income and current savings. Having a large standard deduction would obviate the need to make some consumption categories exempt.

We should insist that wealth taxes stay on the agenda,

---

[15] Terry Barker, 'Taxing pollution instead of employment.' *Energy and Environment* 6 (1993).

particularly so far as inheritance is concerned. Equality of opportunity is not compatible with the unfettered transmission of wealth from generation to generation. Bill Gates's rise to extreme wealth is one thing; allowing such economic privilege to carry on across the generations is not. As in other areas, tax incentives can be mixed with other forms of regulation. Positive incentives for philanthropy, for example, can have as significant a role as taxes on the direct transmission of wealth.

Finally, governments need to work together – as to some extent they already do – to coordinate tax-gathering from multinational companies. Many multinationals engage in tax arbitrage and transfer pricing to limit their international exposure to taxation. Transfer pricing is a critical issue for nation states. Over 80% of multinationals in one study admitted to facing a transfer pricing inquiry from local or foreign tax authorities at some point. The international tax transfer pricing regime that exists at the moment should be tightened up. The existing system is slow, cumbersome and hit and miss.[16]

Will these sources of taxation generate sufficient income for public institutions? No one knows for sure. The problem of securing adequate taxation is unlikely to go away. Citizens will be increasingly reluctant to pay taxes where the revenues aren't being used to their satisfaction, even in those countries that currently sustain higher taxation income than is the norm. The spread of internet

---

[16] Lorraine Eden, *Taxing Multinationals*. Toronto: University of Toronto Press, 1998, p. 635.

business activities, and of e-money, could further exacerbate these problems. Social democrats need to continue to think creatively about taxation, and to connect such thinking with the structural reforms of government and the state mentioned earlier.

Inequality and the welfare state

The need to reform welfare systems is a key part of third way political philosophy. There are three main reasons why. First, existing welfare structures have become out of line with the social and economic changes going on in the world. The dynamics of inequality are different from the past, as are some of the risks to be covered. Women are in the labour market in much larger numbers than before; the relationship between work and family life has changed; there are far more single-parent households; educational needs and possibilities have altered; increasing longevity plus the proliferation of medical treatments are transforming health-care systems and posing many new problems for them. Second, in at least some of its aspects, and in some countries, the welfare state has become unsustainable. Rather than creating greater social solidarity, as it is supposed to do, in this situation welfare institutions can undermine it. As is well known, for example, the pension commitments of some countries, such as Germany, Italy or Japan, are completely unrealizable, even with no further changes at all in demographic trends. Some countries have incurred such a high level of debt that a good deal of taxation simply goes to paying the interest, rather than being spent directly upon welfare services themselves. New social conflicts arise around these strains – taxpayers' revolts, divisions between the generations, struggles between those who do well out of the system and others who do not. Third, as mentioned earlier, the welfare state has its own limitations and contradictions, which need to be tackled in a direct way.

Many books have been written about welfare reform, and the issues involved go far beyond what could be discussed here. I shall concentrate only on some general attributes of welfare restructuring directly relevant to poverty and inequality. The key elements of a third way approach to welfare reform are by now well established. A focus on social exclusion is of prime importance. The notion of social exclusion has come under attack from some on the left, who see it as a means of trying to sweep uncomfortable facts under the carpet. Why talk of exclusion when what we really mean is poverty and deprivation? In fact the idea of social exclusion wasn't invented by third way thinkers or politicians, but by UNESCO and EU researchers. They had a clear rationale for introducing the concept. 'Social exclusion' directs our attention to the social mechanisms that produce or sustain deprivation. Some of these are new, such as the declining demand for male unskilled or semi-skilled workers. Others derive from the welfare state itself (like poverty traps) or from social engineering that went wrong. The most notable examples of the second of these are 'estates on the edge' – housing estates built to help alleviate poverty, but which have instead become areas of social and economic desolation.[17]

Although the term isn't often used in this fashion, I think it is worthwhile talking of social exclusion at the top as well as at the bottom of society. Here again we aren't just describing differences in degree – some people being richer than others – but mechanisms of social, economic and cultural separation. By far their most important manifestation is the withdrawal of elites from commitment to their social and economic responsibilities, including fiscal obligations.

Social exclusion at the bottom is not the same as poverty. The majority of those who are poor at any one time would not be ranked among the excluded. Exclusion contrasts with being 'poor', 'deprived', or 'on a low income' in several ways. It is not a matter of differing from others in degree – having fewer resources – but of not sharing in opportunities that the majority have. In the case of the worst urban areas or neighbourhoods, exclusion can take the form of a physical separation from the rest of society. In other instances it may mean lack of access to normal labour market opportunities. 'The deprived are losers but the excluded do not even take part in the game.'[18]

Exclusion refers to circumstances that affect more or less the entire life of an individual, not just a few aspects of it. As with other situations, however, it is important to see that to be excluded is not always the same as being

[17] Anne Power, *Estates on the Edge*. London: Macmillan, 1997.
[18] Leisering and Leibfried, *Time and Poverty in Western Welfare States*, p. 246.

powerless to influence one's circumstances. The social and economic factors that can lead to exclusion are always filtered through the way individuals react to the problems that confront them.

Countering mechanisms of social exclusion is an emphasis that meshes closely with other themes of third way politics, including that of personal responsibility.

The new social contract, tying rights to responsibilities, has to be built into a reformed welfare system. The catch-phrase of the American New Democrats, that welfare should offer a hand-up, not a hand-out, takes on flesh in the emphasis placed upon labour market reform and job creation. Taxpayers are certainly not 'getting a good enough return' on their investment if large sums are being spent on those out of work when the money could be redirected to areas such as education and health care. This consideration reiterates the fundamental importance of dynamic labour markets that permit good access to jobs. Third way politicians are right to place a prime emphasis on the labour market in welfare reforms, building on the experience of countries that introduced active labour market policies early on. Such reforms need to be conjoined to other strategies of job creation.

The jury is still out on the effects of the 1996 Welfare Reform Act in the US, the central part of Bill Clinton's aim 'to end welfare as we know it'. On the face of things, the results are encouraging. By 1998 nearly 2 million people who had been receiving welfare benefits were in paid work. The proportion of people receiving welfare assistance went down by 27% over that period. The reality is probably more sobering. In some states in the US where workfare schemes have been introduced, only some 30% of people who found jobs were still in them two years later. For some, the problem is the persistence of social exclusion – people are caught up in a cycle of violence, deteriorating family relationships, drugs and alcohol. Others haven't received sufficient education or training to move up a jobs ladder, or to change jobs successfully.

To respond actively to such problems, government needs to be involved across a broader front. The marked element of compulsion in the American system is unlikely to be copied by social democrats elsewhere. Other models of flexibility are available, at least some aspects of which might be capable of generalization. Although they have their limitations, the Dutch welfare reforms show that it is feasible to combine flexibility with high levels of training and retraining, and with a reasonable degree of worker security. About half the jobs generated in the Netherlands from the early to mid-1990s were part-time, but three-quarters of the workers in these jobs had training qualifications. A variety of other forms of 'structured flexibility' can be contemplated. One example is the idea of job rotation. When a worker leaves his or her job, it is kept open for a maximum of a year. He or she can use that year to gain a qualification proposed by the employer. The state guarantees a training and living allowance, fixed at a proportion of the worker's current net pay, funded by savings in unemployment benefits.

Policies designed to counter social exclusion won't be successful if they aren't directed to the changing character of the life course that accompanies the development of the new economy. We should be prepared to be experimental here. As Richard Freeman has remarked, 'Excepting radio talk show hosts, nobody claims certainty about what new policies we need. And given our fundamental uncertainty about how the new economy works, nobody should.'[19] At present, most social programmes deal with overall categories of people, such as the 'unemployed' or the 'homeless'. But this approach is not particularly useful, since there are such large variations in how long periods of poverty last, and how they are experienced. One possibility might be to have different policies in relation to duration. For instance, it has been suggested that government loans could be given to those who are temporarily poor, and to people who move in and out of poverty repeatedly. Their needs are quite different from those of the long-term poor.[20]

Another possibility might be to shift redistribution forward in the life course, concentrating upon the young. The virtues of child allowances, parental leave, day-care provisions and expenditure on pre-school education have been well demonstrated in the countries that have them. Other asset-based transfers are worth considering, however, such as the proposal that every young person might receive a voucher after leaving school that could be redeemed in further education or training.

[19] Richard Freeman, *The New Inequality: Creating Solutions for Poor America*. Boston: Beacon, 1999, p. 12.
[20] Leisering and Leibfried, *Time and Poverty in Western Welfare States*, p. 259.

'Wherever possible invest in human capital' strongly suggests an enabling approach to social policy – building upon the action strategies of the poor. Such an approach again fits closely with a stress upon initiative and responsibility. The finding that most welfare claimants are much more active than was previously believed might be thought to imply that state support for them should be reduced or eliminated. The real conclusion that should be drawn is the opposite – the fact that most claimants actively look for ways to become independent shows that investing in them pays.

The same point applies to those who have no chance of getting from welfare to work – children, the disabled or sick, the elderly and others. There should be no suggestion that they should be penalized as part of the transition from passive to active welfare policies. But it still makes sense to help mobilize their action potential and reduce dependency. Social policy in some such contexts has to be connected to other policy endeavours – such as improving facilities for the disabled and tackling prejudice against them.

The first researcher to concentrate upon the life cycle in relation to poverty and inequality was closely involved with the policy initiatives of the New Democrats – David Ellwood, a Harvard professor who worked with Bill Clinton's welfare reform initiative. Besides collecting time-series data for the initiative, Ellwood directly studied welfare offices and interviewed welfare officials and recipients. The welfare system, he concluded – not only in the US, but in Europe too – concentrates on the 'who' of poverty, not the 'why'. One welfare recipient said,

'I've been on and off welfare for ten years. I've been in and out of the welfare office dozens of times. Never once in that entire ten-year period did anyone ask me what I always thought would be the first question, "What's the problem, how can I help you?" Instead they say, "What's your income? How many kids do you have?"'[21]

Research is starting to tell us more about the 'why'. In studying social assistance claimants in Germany, Lutz Leisering and Stephan Leibfried distinguish several different modes of responding to poverty.[22] They stress that 'coping strategies' have to be looked at broadly: living with poverty is about more than only being poor.

Only a limited number of people, they say, experience poverty as 'victims'. These are individuals who feel trapped in poverty, particularly as a result of long-term unemployment. They have found it impossible to get a job, and have given up looking. Since they can't find a way forward through their own efforts, they accept dependence on welfare benefits. Their encounters with the welfare system serve to confirm their feelings that they cannot achieve anything on their own.

Those whom the researchers call 'survivors' develop more active 'social assistance careers'. Long-term unemployment is the main problem for this group too. Unlike

---

[21] David Ellwood, 'Dynamic policy making: an insider's account of reforming US welfare.' In *The Dynamics of Modern Society*, ed. Lutz Leisering and Robert Walker. Bristol: Policy Press, 1998, p. 51.

[22] Leisering and Leibfried, *Time and Poverty in Western Welfare States*, p. 239.

the 'victims', however, their relationship with the social assistance agency has not become problematic. They manage to deal with some of their difficulties, and keep the hope of finding a job alive.

'Pragmatic copers' treat social assistance as a means to wider ends. They are pursuing life goals over and above adapting to limited economic resources. Unemployment is less significant for these individuals who are facing problems such as marital separation and single parenthood. They put up with the restrictions of claiming and their dependency on the welfare agency without too much difficulty.

People who actively sustain more long-term ambitions are 'biographical copers'. They plan for the future, and are prepared to change their attitudes and strategies to pursue their goals. For example, one woman the researchers interviewed left her alcoholic husband following the birth of their second child. She planned to take up vocational training as soon as her children were old enough, and found that social assistance gave her a degree of autonomy she had not had before. She was later able to pursue a highly successful career in education.

'Strategic users' have a more instrumental attitude still. They deploy social assistance as one resource among others to achieve a certain style of life. For them, claiming is almost wholly unproblematic, a means of income that can be supplemented by other sources, illegally in some cases. They may have chosen to be unemployed, at least for a period, in order to pursue other concerns or interests. All of these groups, Leisering and Leibfried found,

were internally quite heterogeneous. 'The new insight is
. . . that poverty has many faces.'[23]

Leisering and Leibfried speak of Germany as a '70–
20–10' society and, allowing for variations in these per-
centages, much the same label could be applied to most
other industrial countries: 70% of the population have
never been poor, 20% have or will occasionally be in
poverty, while 10% are poor in a more chronic fashion.

Taking a dynamic, life-chances approach to inequality
means above all ensuring that poverty isn't a permanent
condition. We need to minimize situations where either
poverty brings about social exclusion, or social exclusion causes chronic poverty. The new poverty research
drives home the fact that countering social exclusion
means tackling inequality on a wide front. The life circumstances of others than the immediate poor need to
be improved or protected, because otherwise short-term
periods of deprivation can become more permanent.
Those at risk include people in apparently secure jobs
and social positions that might once have made them relatively immune. A woman might be 'only a divorce away'
from impoverishment, perhaps along with her children –
this could be true even if she were the instigator of the
divorce.

People living more or less permanently on low incomes,
especially when only one member of a family is working,
are vulnerable. Their difficulties may stem not so much
from the threat of unemployment as such, as from their

---

[23] Leisering and Leibfried, *Time and Poverty in Western Welfare States*, p. 242.

inability to build up a stock of savings should things go wrong. They may have no capital assets at all, and can become pushed over into poverty should they face even relatively small crises.

Some such groups on the edge of poverty are caught in a 'low-pay, no-pay cycle' – getting into low-paid jobs does not result in stable employment. This fact suggests that policy-makers should place more emphasis on how people develop from their first job. Policies relevant to such an objective could involve counselling for career development, plus interventions in local labour markets. These interventions would need to focus upon specific features of low-paid jobs. For instance, to employers low-paid jobs might signal low productivity and hence 'disposable labour'. Some low-paid jobs might have the effect of deskilling people.[24] Government-provided assistance or incentive schemes could help meet such problems.

The long-term poor

There can be no question of 'explaining away' the importance of chronic poverty as a fundamental constraint upon the lives of those exposed to it. Conservative writers are fond of arguing that 'poverty is not an excuse' for those who do not fare well, since some exceptional individuals from even the most deprived backgrounds do become successes. But they succeed precisely because they are exceptional, not because their experiences can be gen-

[24] Oxley, 'Poverty dynamics in four OECD countries'.

eralized to those of the majority. Enduring poverty is usually coupled to exclusionary mechanisms, and hence affects most aspects of life. Children born in such circumstances are often deprived even before they first emerge into the world. Their mothers may suffer from inadequate nutrition and are likely to have inferior prenatal care compared with the more affluent. Children from deprived backgrounds are several times more likely to have physical disabilities and be abused or neglected. Their disadvantages carry on through their education, or lack of it. Schools in poor neighbourhoods are often underfunded, staffed by demoralized teachers, who have to concern themselves with keeping control in the classroom rather than with instruction.

Specific help is needed for the long-term poor, but – as with welfare provision more generally – it isn't necessary or desirable that it should come only from government. Innovative policies are likely to involve a mixture of agencies. Consider as an example Michael Porter's work on the competitive advantage of the inner city.[25] Most European cities have not experienced a flight to the suburbs on the part of the more affluent, as the US has. Yet, particularly where immigrant populations are involved, many of the same problems of inner-city decay and criminality appear in Europe.

Looking at different cases from across the US, Porter shows that, in spite of the deployment of considerable

---

[25] Michael Porter, 'The competitive advantage of the inner city.' In *On Competition*. Cambridge, MA: Harvard Business Review Books, 1998, pp. 377–408.

government resources, efforts to establish a sustainable economic base in the inner cities have not been successful. Support for the inner cities has mostly consisted of welfare programmes, housing subsidies, food stamps and other piecemeal provisions. Intervention directed at promoting economic development has normally sought to assist small businesses, or foster services oriented to local neighbourhoods.

Some such endeavours are unquestionably not only useful, but essential. Yet they don't provide an effective overall strategy for development and renewal. To forge such a strategy, Porter argues, we should take a radically different approach. Inner-city business could and should be positioned to compete in regional, national and even international markets. We should seek to redistribute wealth by means of creating new wealth.

What competitive advantages do inner cities have that might be turned to such ends? Porter identifies four: strategic location, local market demand, integration with regional clusters, and human resources. Inner cities sit in geographical areas that should be prized – think of the proximity of London's East End to the financial centres of the City. Market opportunities are present because, at a time when other markets tend to be saturated, inner-city markets are poorly served – in retailing, banking, or personal services, for example. Average incomes may be low, but because the density of population is usually high, there is substantial spending power available.

Capitalizing on major regional clusters offers inner-city areas access to competitive companies and resources. Porter believes that this is one of the most significant, yet unexploited, sources of local economic growth. Where there are developed industries nearby, companies providing supplies, components and support services could be created to take advantage of the proximity of the inner city to nearby customers. Most inner-city residents want to work, and are industrious. It is a myth that the only entrepreneurs in inner cities are drug-dealers. Local entrepreneurs are often already active in the social sector. They can use their expertise to develop economically competitive enterprises as well as social ones.

Obviously there are many barriers to inner-city development too – a low level of communications, high material costs, poor security, lack of employee skills, limited access to debt and equity capital. Like Moss Kanter, Porter looks to new forms of collaboration between business, government and the non-profit sector to overcome some of these problems. Government needs to contribute, but should also recognize that its own initiatives can inhibit needed changes. Government resources should be used to provide extra security, help refurbishment and environmental clean-up and other investments that create an effective economic milieu.

Social exclusion at the top

Coping with social exclusion at the top is just as important as efforts to counter poverty. It is as complex too. 'The rich' are no more of a homogeneous category than 'the poor'. Moreover wealth, like poverty, has to be considered in life-cycle terms. 'The rich' includes families with long-standing wealth, captains of industry, investment bankers and shareholders, rentiers, celebrities and sportsmen, among many others. Some may have become affluent early in life, others much later. People who have been wealthy might lose some or all of it, or hover around the edges of wealth, however that may be defined. Wealth as much as poverty has many faces.

In seeking to limit social and economic polarization, therefore, no single strategy will do. Policies, including the adjustment of taxation systems, need to be tailored to context. Yet we can fairly easily identify some of the main questions involved. Among the more important are how to contain sheer economic inequality, how to promote a sense of civic obligation and commitment, and how to prevent mechanisms of social exclusion from developing.

Progressive income, wealth and inheritance taxes, plus incentives for philanthropy, as noted before, must play a basic role so far as the first of these issues is concerned. But for some groups of the wealthy, other taxation issues are just as relevant – such as those governing stock options, tax expenditures or tax havens. In addition, with intensifying globalization there seem to be new sources of economic inequality at the top in some contexts, and these aren't easy to counter. One is the expansion of winner-take-all markets.

Winner-take-all markets are structural. They aren't the same as the use of corporate power to accumulate personal rewards. The winner-take-all effect comes from the fact that small differences at the very top in labour markets are highly consequential. A star tennis player may be only slightly better than his or her rivals, but that small difference produces vastly greater earning power. A champion on the world professional tennis tour can earn millions; someone ranked a hundred places below, who is very nearly as good, might struggle to make only a modest living from the game.

Government can't and shouldn't do much about winner-take-all markets when they operate appropriately. But they don't always do so. There is little public resentment against the earnings of sports stars, presumably because people accept that there is open, non-monopolistic competition. They don't see things quite in the same way when the directors of large corporations are paid vast salaries. The intuition of the public is surely correct. Directors of companies can use their positions to reward themselves economically, and corporate salaries by no means always correlate closely with the actual performance of firms.

It is in principle, and to a large degree in practice, possible to disentangle winner-take-all effects from the influence of monopolistic power – or, not to put too fine a point on it, boardroom greed. The winner in competitive sports gives evidence of his or her worth by the very fact of victory. Comparable evidence should be demanded in the spheres of finance and industry – where possible, by government, and where necessary, by shareholder activist groups. Boardroom rewards should correspond to the success or otherwise of companies.

The originators of the idea of winner-take-all markets, Robert Frank and Philip Cook, suggest a number of further ways of limiting the inequalities that such markets create.[26] One, that converges with developments in the field of taxation suggested earlier, is progressive consumption taxes. Progressive consumption taxes make entry into winner-take-all competitions less attractive, thus limiting the inegalitarian outcomes. A progressive consumption tax could be constructed to be in effect a luxury tax. Social and cultural factors, however, are also relevant. Derek Bok, for example, lays emphasis upon the social ratification of greed that was fostered by the ideological climate of neoliberalism in the 1980s.[27] As we move away from a neoliberal outlook, it may be that such cultural attitudes will fade too – especially if combined with tougher controls.

The civic concerns of elites are plainly not separate from questions of taxation; avoiding taxes, or pulling out all the stops to pay as little tax as possible, are at the same time evasions of civic duty. However, obligation and commitment go well beyond fiscal responsibilities. Those moralists who make extensive civic demands upon welfare recipients would do well to make them also of business leaders and other elite groups. A social contract of mutual obligation, as emphasized earlier, must stretch from bottom to top. Many business leaders do not act as full citizens, since they ignore the social outcomes of their business decisions. Benjamin Barber speaks of this as 'corporate schizophrenia'. As he puts it, 'the wall between public and private sectors has insulated corporations and

[26] Robert H. Frank and Philip J. Cook, *The Winner-Take-All Society*. New York: Free Press, 1995.
[27] Derek Bok, *The Cost of Talent*. New York: Free Press, 1993.

their personnel from civic responsibility and allowed this corporate schizophrenia to insulate their men and women, whether employers or employees, from their obligations as citizens'.[28]

Acceptance of civic obligation is not in turn separate from social segregation – inhabiting a private and exclusive world, separate from the experience of the majority of the population. How can this situation be prevented? There is one main way, and that is by making sure that public institutions remain legitimate, robust and effective – including the welfare state. A tiny elite of the extremely rich will no doubt always live in its own world. More important for social concerns are again the 'merely affluent'. If state schools and medical services are good, city centres kept refurbished and crime contained, the motivation to retreat on the part of those who can afford to do so will be much less.

Conclusion

The distinctive qualities of a third way approach to inequality are easy to summarize. Such an approach concerns itself both with equality and pluralism, placing an emphasis on a dynamic model of egalitarianism. It focuses primarily upon equality of opportunity, but stresses that this also presumes economic redistribution. It seeks to respond to changing influences upon inequality as well as to its changing patterns. The state, including the wel-

[28] Barber, *A Place For Us*, p. 95.

fare state, it is argued, does not just 'react to' inequality and to poverty. It enters into the life circumstances of individuals and groups involved.

The restructuring of welfare systems should have several ends in view – saving on costs where necessary, but also reacting to new social and economic conditions and coping with the perverse outcomes to which the welfare state has given rise. Social and economic policy can no longer be treated as though they were in separate compartments. Social spending has to be assessed in terms of its consequences for the economy as a whole – one of the reasons for the prominent role given to welfare-to-work policies. Social exclusion should be examined and reacted to both at the bottom and the top. Redefining inequality in relation to exclusion at both levels is consistent with a dynamic view of deprivation and privilege.

As in other areas of political policy, inequality can't be dealt with only on a national plane. Issues of global economic governance, and the regulation of corporate power, have to be confronted in a direct way too, problematic and complicated though they might be. These issues form the substance of the concluding chapters.

5

Taking Globalization Seriously

As a globalizing political philosophy, third way politics should look to promote further global integration, in full cognizance of how difficult this may be, and without being naive or sanguine about the possibilities before us. Modernizing social democrats have to come to grips with the transitions taking place in world society. Since the advance of globalization is so much stronger than it has been before, it makes sense to suppose that the global order is different from the past. The very name and definition of 'international relations' has become outdated, as most scholars in the field now stress.

Nation states remain the most important agents on the international scene. The turnover of the biggest multinational companies might be bigger than the GDP of most states, but nation states are still generically much more powerful. The reasons are that they control territory, whereas corporations don't; they can legitimately wield military force, whether individually or collectively; and they are responsible, again either individually or on a collective level, for sustaining an apparatus of law. Yet the global system cannot today be described or analysed just on the level of nations, because nations and their claims to sovereignty are being so radically reshaped. In addition to the powerful influences of the global marketplace and new communications technology, there is a groundswell of 'globalization from below', involving many millions of ordinary people as well as organized groups of all kinds. An infrastructure of global civil society is being built by these changes. It can be indexed by the growing number of non-governmental organizations. In 1950 there were only two or three hundred. Now there are more than 10,000 and the trend is still sharply upwards.

What kind of global developments should third way activists seek to promote? Abstractly, the answer to this question is the same as on the local or national levels. A healthy global order would achieve a balance between government, the economy and civil society. As long as these are out of kilter, world society will remain unstable. We do not have an effective balance at the moment. The global economy, and the accompanying processes of technological change, are swamping nascent forms of governance, which need to be much strengthened. In many countries, and some regions, there is as yet no developed civil society, and hence little democracy; without these there is little chance of effective economic development either.

In a speech given in Chicago in April 1999 Tony Blair stated, on behalf of third way social democracy, 'we are all internationalists now, whether we like it or not. We cannot refuse to participate in global markets if we want to prosper. We cannot ignore new political ideas in other countries if we want to innovate. We cannot turn our backs on conflicts and the violation of human rights if we still want to be secure.'[1] He was surely right in these emphases. If we take globalization seriously, as certainly we must, national policies have to become more thoroughly integrated with global perspectives.

Modernizing social democrats should encourage international collaboration on several fronts. There are five basic areas where global institutions need to be strengthened or further developed: the governance of the world economy, global ecological management, the regulation of corporate power, the control of warfare and the fostering of transnational democracy. All pose formidable problems, but in each area growing global integration suggests feasible solutions or approaches. In the remainder of this chapter I shall discuss them in turn.

Global economic governance

Economic globalization, by and large, has been a success. The problem is how to maximize its positive consequences while limiting its less fortunate effects. The overall success of economic globalization isn't difficult to confirm. Over the last twenty years, in spite of the high levels of unemployment that exist in some countries and regions, the absolute amount of employment in the world has

---

[1] Tony Blair, 'Doctrine of the international community.' Speech at the Hilton Hotel, Chicago (22 April 1999).

expanded dramatically. The global labour force grew by some 630 million between 1980 and 1994, far outstripping population growth.

In this period, the Chinese economy alone generated more than 15 million new net jobs per year. In spite of recent setbacks, the rapid economic development of the Asian economies has lifted millions of people out of poverty. The improvement in living conditions that has been brought about is shown by improvements in infant mortality and life expectancy. Infant mortality in South Korea was 62 per thousand in 1965, but only 12 per thousand in 1994. Life expectancy rose from 54 to 71 years. In China, the comparable figures were 90 per thousand in 1965, and 30 per thousand in 1994. Average life expectancy in China rose from 47 to 69 years. As Mauricio Rojas says, 'what the unparalleled advances of the past 30 years have shown is that our new global economy has an enormous potential, that there is an alternative to poverty and underdevelopment, that the thing now is to transform more and more countries into dynamic parts of this expansive economy'.[2]

Yet the world cannot afford a repeat of the East Asian crisis with all the knock-on consequences it has had in Russia and elsewhere. That crisis was not a unique one, although it was the most far-reaching. It followed earlier financial crises in the 1980s in Latin America, the European exchange rate difficulties of 1992 and the Mexican bond crisis of 1994. The common thread in all of these

---

[2] Mauricio Rojas, *Millennium Doom*. London: Social Market Foundation, 1999, p. 12.

was the volatile nature of capital flows. What happened resembled financial panics of earlier times, but took place with greater speed, scope and intensity because of the instantaneous character of global market reactions today. It isn't only that there can be a sudden surge of capital out of a country or area – capital can rush into favoured hot spots as well. Both processes have undesirable effects. The damage produced by rapid outflows of money has been evident in each successive crisis. But surges of capital inwards can also have destabilizing effects, leading to the over-valuation of exchange rates, rising property and asset prices, and a bubble economy.

Several sorts of policy measures could be taken to stabilize the global monetary system.[3] Each is provided for only to a limited degree by existing institutional arrangements.

One is the development of appropriate regulations providing for surveillance of financial transactions. In order to monitor such transactions effectively, a specialized agency might need to be established – a world financial authority. Its main task would be the management of systemic risk in the world financial economy. It should also contribute to developing rules for international financial cooperation. The main capital flows that need further regulation, and seem to have been implicated in each of the recent crises, are short-term bank loans, portfolio flows – such as hedge funds – and derivatives.

A second is the provision of official international li-

---

[3] Stephany Griffith-Jones, 'A new financial architecture for reducing risks and severity of crises.' *International Politics & Society* 3 (1999).

quidity for specific countries or financial markets, with particular attention given to creating an adequate lender of last resort. Response to a currency crisis needs to be fast, since even in two or three weeks major damage can be done to an economy or economies on the receiving end. One suggestion is that a country's right to borrow could be established in advance. The country would draw on this resource only if a crisis occurred, but could do so immediately.

National economies have a lender of last resort, in the shape of a central bank. The global economy urgently needs some parallel institutions too. At present such institutions simply do not exist. While the International Monetary Fund has become increasingly important, it cannot create unlimited liquidity and only lends conditionally. The ultimate aim should surely be to set up a global central bank. But in the meantime it may be possible to perform some of its functions with less ambitious organizations. A revised and expanded IMF could work alongside a facility for more broad-based lending.

The third element is the provision of orderly, official channels for the workout of debts. The scale of recent rescue packages from the IMF in Asia and elsewhere has given rise to serious problems of moral hazard. Where it is accepted that a country which gets into financial difficulties will be bailed out, investors are likely to adjust their assessment of risk accordingly, as might that country's government. Means need to be found to ensure greater risk-bearing by private investors, as well as to involve the private sector early on in processes of crisis resolution. Various possibilities exist. Bonds issued in sovereign offerings could incorporate contractual changes giving debt-holders rights of representation in the event of a crisis and require a sharing of repayments among creditors. Where a temporary suspension of payment is allowed, cooperative and orderly restructuring, with appropriate reforms, could be made a condition.

The steering mechanisms for the global economy that exist at the moment are heavily weighted towards the richer countries – in particular those major industrial democracies which form the G7 and G8 groups. Brazil, which has a GDP of some $800 billion, has less formal power than Sweden, with a GDP of well under a third of that figure. A grouping established in September 1999 will redress the imbalance somewhat. The new group, GX, includes the G7 countries together with China, India, Brazil, Russia, Mexico, South Korea, and South Africa. It is at least possible that GX could become the most significant institution for overall global economic steering. GX will have a permanent status, and will coordinate its work with G7 and the IMF.

Such innovations are important, since the gap between the richest and poorest countries in the world is huge. Over the past thirty years, income per capita in the developing countries has on average grown faster than in the industrial societies. But the countries at the bottom of the economic scale have had growth rates that are either zero or negative. In 1965 the average income per capita in the G7 countries was twenty times that in the poorest seven countries. By 1997 the ratio was 40 to 1. To find a true economic comparison, these figures have to be adjusted for the differences in the cost of living, which brings down the differential considerably. But it is still very high.

Social democratic leaders should collaborate to declare a global war on poverty for the first twenty years of the new century. The idea of taxing speculative currency transactions, first floated many years ago, should be properly examined and debated. An onslaught on poverty would demand large-scale investment in human capital and infrastructure, linked to social and political criteria as much as economic considerations. Even were they possible, large transfer payments of cash to the poorer nations would make quite a small impact on their own. It has been calculated that if 75% of the income per head of the developed societies were redistributed to the poorer countries, the average income in those countries would only go up by 20%.[4]

Most of the problems that inhibit the economic development of the impoverished countries don't come from the global economy itself, or from self-seeking behaviour on the part of the richer nations. They lie mainly in the societies themselves – in authoritarian government, corruption, conflict, over-regulation and the low level of emancipation of women. Mobile investment capital will give such countries a wide berth, since the level of risk is unacceptable.

It is difficult indeed to make breakthroughs where such circumstances take the form of a vicious circle. Resources coming from the outside, however, can help trigger the

[4] Robin Marris, *Ending Poverty*. London: Thames & Hudson, 1999, p. 105.

necessary indigenous changes, and if correctly invested offer the chance of development for even the most deprived. Directing investment to human resources, promoting active supply interventions, and coupling these with structural changes in state and civil society – these are even more crucial in the less developed countries than in the more economically advanced ones.

These points bring us back to freedom as social capability, as defined by Sen. Economic development, he argues, cannot be assessed without reference to the contributions that health and education, civil and political freedoms make to human well-being. The capabilities approach measures development in terms of literacy, the ability to express oneself freely, to vote, and to be free from the fear of violence or persecution. Capabilities are not only 'intrinsically' important, but 'instrumentally' so as well. In Sen's view, a country's development can be best advanced by developing civil and political rights and by investing in health care and education. The idea that these are luxuries that can be deferred until more basic economic growth is achieved is quite wrong. Democracy, he says, is the best safeguard against famine – no fully-fledged democracy has ever experienced major famine.[5]

Overseas aid can help, especially where used as a stimulus to internal reform. When private investment flows were at their height, many came to consider direct development assistance superfluous. Following the Asian cri-

---

[5] Amartya Sen, *Development as Freedom*. Oxford: Oxford University Press, 1999.

sis, however, private investment to developing countries all but dried up. Building the infrastructure necessary for democracy and an effective market economy demands aid provided and supported by overseas governments.

Aid has been successful in the past provided certain basic conditions are met. It must be used in conjunction with domestically sound social and economic policies, and it must reach groups able to promote these policies. As World Bank statistics show, in such situations 1% assistance in GDP translates into an equivalent percentage decline in poverty and infant mortality.[6] Moreover, given these provisos there is no evidence that aid 'crowds out' other sources of finance. On the contrary, investors tend to be reassured if reform processes go hand in hand with foreign aid.

These points imply that aid should be channelled towards governments and other agencies that show commitment and expertise in working for the disadvantaged. A shift in world aid spending patterns would help, directed to poor countries that – against the odds – have begun to build effective government and the conditions for market exchange to flourish. Examples include Mozambique, Mali and Bangladesh. According to Ethan Kapstein, if all donor countries made such 'poverty-efficient' distributions of aid, 80 million people a year would be lifted out of subsistence poverty.[7] Even existing allocations of aid, which are low and badly targeted, have this outcome for 30 million people each year.

[6] World Bank, *Assessing Aid*. New York: Oxford University Press, 1998.
[7] Ethan B. Kapstein, 'Reviving aid.' *World Policy Journal* (Fall 1999).

Some worthwhile initiatives are being taken. In September 1999 the richer countries agreed to write off much of the money owed to creditors by the world's poorer societies. The British Chancellor of the Exchequer Gordon Brown spoke of forming a 'worldwide alliance against poverty' in the new century. It was proposed that a coordinated attempt be made to meet the UN target of halving world poverty by 2015.

Global ecological management

The ecological problems the world faces are at least as challenging as those posed by global inequalities. Yet we need not be as pessimistic about them as we might have been a few years ago, when it was widely assumed that economic development and sound ecological management are incompatible. Applying strict environmental standards seemed to mean that businesses must shoulder the costs of ecological improvements; these costs produce higher prices and a loss of competitiveness. Ecological agencies and industry appeared inevitably in conflict. Where the arguments are framed in this fashion 'progress on environmental quality [becomes] a kind of arm-wrestling match. One side pushes for tougher standards; the other to roll them back. The balance of power shifts one way or the other depending on the prevailing political winds.'[8]

---

[8] Michael Porter, 'Green and competitive.' In *On Competition*, p. 351.

The new orientation towards ecological modernization takes a quite different tack. An ecologically sophisticated outlook can promote innovations that allow producers to function more efficiently, enhancing resource productivity. There are many examples. Thus in 1992 Greenpeace in Germany endorsed an environmentally safer agent for cooling refrigerators than was then generally in use. The organization backed a commercial product for the first time in its history, and even ran an advertising campaign for it. The system proved cheaper and more effective than the existing alternatives, and later most producers made the shift to the same technology.

Another illustration comes from the Dutch flower industry, where until recently intensive methods of cultivation, using pesticides and fertilizers, were contaminating the soil. The producers then introduced a closed-loop system, in which flowers grow in water and rock wool rather than soil. Product quality was improved and handling costs lowered, improving the competitiveness of the industry.

Of course, in many cases there is no such virtuous circle, but there is reason to suppose that it applies more often than not. Pollution is ecologically hazardous, but it is also a form of economic waste; waste is a sign that resources have been used incompletely or inefficiently. In addition, waste usually generates add-on costs, since additional cleansing procedures have to be carried out that create no extra economic value. Ecological programmes have normally concentrated on pollution control; in place of this, more advanced regulators and businesses are using methods that prevent or limit pollution before it occurs. Environmental hazards are seen as reflecting inefficient design, not as inevitable by-products of processes of manufacture.

The waste industry exemplifies the changes that need to be made. Thus in the UK 435 million tonnes of waste is disposed of every year.[9] Only a small portion is domestic waste. Some 85% comes from commercial and industrial activities. Much of this is simply processed and buried. The whole industry, however, is becoming transformed. Technological developments make it much cheaper to produce newsprint from recycled paper than from wood pulp. Glass factories are now able to use some 90% recycled materials. Not just companies, but whole industries, are actively pursuing the goal of zero waste. Toyota and Honda have reached a level of 85% recyclability for the car parts they use. Waste is no longer waste, but a resource for industry and a driver of innovation.

Significantly, some of the major contributions to recycling have come from the areas with IT industries, especially Silicon Valley in California. In principle, the knowledge economy has quite different environmental implications from the industrial one. Industrial manufacture used to be resource-intensive – like the agricultural economy that preceded it. In the new economy, economic development no longer means using more physical resources to produce more. It means instead producing more with less.

Some have suggested that with the advent of the know-

[9] Robin Murray, *Creating Wealth from Waste*. London: Demos, 1999.

ledge economy it will be possible to produce twice as much, using half the material resources we do at the moment.[10] The principle of 'factor four' applies even within the computer industry itself. Hard-disk drives made some five years ago use ten times more energy than more recent ones, which are actually more powerful. Small computers which use only a few watts can be as powerful as 150-watt desktop computers. Most computers are unused for about 90% of the time when they are switched on. The introduction of a device that puts the computer into hibernation until it is needed again saved some 70% of the energy required and the life of the computer was extended. Before this and other innovations, desktop computers needed fans to cool them. Once the power supply and the chips it ran became more efficient, the fan could be dispensed with.

Technological advance in these instances appears as a positive force, but plainly this isn't always so. The development of science and technology is deeply bound up with questions of risk. Risk is a distinctly double-edged phenomenon. It is the source of economic energy and of most forms of innovation, including those of a scientific or technological kind. Yet by its very nature it presumes the possibility of harmful consequences. Now that the pace of scientific and technological evolution in some areas has become so fast, we have to cope with risk situations that are different in character from those of the past.

---

[10] Ernst Ulrich von Weizsäcker, Amory B. Lovins and L. Hunter Lovins, *Factor Four*. London: Earthscan, 1997.

Take as an example one of the most momentous forms of technological development happening in current times – the merging of information technology and biology.[11] For three or four decades, developments in computers and telecommunications ran separately from those in the life sciences. These are now beginning to fuse into a single body of knowledge and technology, linked to new economic opportunities. Genetic resources can be exploited for social and economic ends by using recombinant DNA techniques. The mapping of the 100,000 or so genes that comprise the human genome, together with developments in genetic screening, makes possible even the alteration of the human species itself. The globalizing of science means that these innovations are not confined to any one country.

Any genetically engineered product that can reproduce poses potential dangers to natural ecosystems. The area where this has been most discussed so far is that of genetically modified foods. Those who say that current techniques are simply an extension of earlier forms of cross-breeding are wrong or disingenuous, since for the first time a variety of transgenic crops can be produced.

The issues involved in responding to such innovations are not essentially different from those that figure in more familiar areas of environmental debate. All are strongly influenced by globalization. Global warming and the depletion of the ozone layer are other obvious examples of ecological issues that are world-wide in their scope and consequences. If global warming is actually happening –

[11] Jeremy Rifkin, *The Biotech Century*. Westlake: J. P. Tarcher, 1999.

and the majority of scientists now think it is – it will affect all continents. The thesis of global warming remains difficult to assess, partly because it is difficult to measure, and partly because detailed monitoring of the earth's climate has only been carried on over the past two or three decades. The consequences are also extremely hard to predict with any precision because of the complex character of the interaction of temperature change with other aspects of climate and other ecological systems and because there are so many unknowns. The shrinking of the ozone layer has a number of similar features. Apart from its implications for human and animal health, it may have diverse consequences of other kinds.

As the progress of science and technology accelerates, we have to get used to dealing with such risk situations – risks that have little precedent in human history. These situations have some distinctive features. We can't make risk assessments in an actuarial way, since there is no prior time-series to go on. The very existence of risk is likely to be disputed, let alone the ramifications that might stem from it. Thus although most climate scientists now agree that global warming is happening, and that it has human origins, there are some who dispute both these claims.

Government can't stand outside processes of risk assessment and the provision of information about them on the basis that such decisions need to be 'left to the experts'. The experts themselves will normally be divided about what the risks are. Public authorities have to be responsible for deciding, not just how to respond to new risk situations, but also when and how to announce that they exist, as well as how they should be debated. If the authorities proclaim a particular risk too early on, and that risk turns out to be either non-existent or lower than was originally imagined, the government will be said to have been scaremongering. Where on the other hand the authorities wait too long, they will be accused of a cover-up. There is also the phenomenon of 'information exhaustion'. The risks associated with global warming, for example, have been so widely propagated that people may become weary of hearing about them and hence desensitized to the dangers involved.

Some environmentalists argue that the most effective response to ecological risk is the adoption of a precautionary principle. Like sustainable development, the idea is often stated only in a vague fashion. Sometimes it seems to imply a generalized hostility to science and technology as such. More rationally, it means either taking action before risks are conclusively established, or resisting developments that contravene 'nature'. The first of these, plainly, is often necessary. We have to act to counter global warming for example, even though its existence has not been conclusively demonstrated. The second, however, is incoherent. It is too late to stay close to nature, even if we should wish to, since so much that happens in the physical environment today is the result of our own interventions, intended and unintended. Take the controversy over genetically modified foods. Those who are opposed to them feel the level of interference with 'nature' GM crops involve is unwarranted, since we don't know in advance what the consequences will be. Yet genetically modified foods offer potential benefits that have to be brought into the equation, and which it is foolish simply to write off. We are always forced back on risk assessment – the balance of dangers and benefits that scientific and technological development offers.

One way of pragmatically assessing risks – that has the advantage of being coupled to a response mechanism – is in terms of liability. Who is to provide cover if technological innovation produces harmful consequences? At the moment, risk and liability are for the most part separate. For many ecological risks, government is assumed to be the 'insurer of last resort'. A more effective approach would be for the innovators to be obliged in law to accept greater liability for what they do. Companies that produce and design GM foods could be made liable for environmental or health damage they might cause – as to a limited extent they already are. Since insurance companies are reluctant to cover a risk with so many unknowns, a brake would be put on irresponsible practices.

More generally, however, we should seek to democratize science and technology, as part of the project of 'democratizing democracy'. We aren't used to treating ecological questions under the rubric of democracy, since problems to do with science and technology are supposed to be resolved by experts. The result of the ever more pervasive influence of scientific and technological development upon our lives, however, is that science can't be left to the scientists. Democratizing such development has to be a major preoccupation of third way politics.

It is a process that needs to happen at a transnational level as well as more locally. The state, however, can have an important role; and such a change can in turn contribute to its own restructuring. As in other areas, governments need to work with social movements and special interest groups, in an open dialogic fashion. Expertise needs to be demonopolized, and negotiating between decision-makers and experts turned into a public encounter, involving a wide range of people. It is not good enough to do this only after the event, as happened in the UK both with the BSE crisis and the controversy over genetically modified foods. Regulatory bodies should be in place that track scientific and technological developments, with a view to anticipating the public debates that should ensue. They should play a part in making those debates informed and accessible, as well as situating them in the wider framework of democratic institutions and the law.

Ecological issues, of course, reflect global inequalities. An easy means of demonstrating this is by adjusting population figures to reflect energy consumption. The population of the United States, at some 250 million people, is a long way behind those of India and China, with 900 million and 1,100 million respectively. If population is adjusted by consumption, however, the figures are entirely different. In terms of consumption-adjusted population, the US exceeds India and China combined by 70%.[12]

The theme of ecological modernization, however, is relevant on a world level as well as a national one. It

---

[12] Commission on Global Governance, *Our Global Neighbourhood*. Oxford: Oxford University Press, 1995.

does not follow that because the developed countries have caused a great deal of ecological damage, less developed ones must go through the same process in order to achieve economic growth themselves. High rates of economic development in the future for poorer countries as well as richer ones might depend increasingly on technologies that are intrinsically non-polluting, or which involve a high degree of recycling.

Moreover, the relation between environmental damage and level of economic advancement is complicated. Some forms of environmental pollution decline with rising living standards, such as the level of suspended particles in urban air. Certain other types of environmental damage seem to follow a u-curve. In the early stages of economic development there is a deterioration in ecological quality, but after a certain point there is a sharp movement upwards again.[13]

A mixture of policy initiatives is called for to cope with these complexities. Global warming will have consequences for all countries, but the societies of the South are most vulnerable. The policy agreements that have so far been forged at a world level are insufficient and look likely to be insufficiently observed. According to the Kyoto Protocol, greenhouse gas emissions should be cut by 8% in the EU, 7% in the US and 6% in Japan early in the new century. Even supposing these targets are met, global warming is likely to continue unless more far-reaching cuts are made. The highest levels of growth in

[13] Gilles Bertrand et al., *Scenarios Europe 2010*. Brussels: European Commission, 1999, pp. 71–3.

emissions are in developing countries, with China and India now contributing one-sixth of the world's total.

Besides binding international agreements which recognize the needs of the developing countries, indigenous changes will need to be made. That national and local policies can also make a difference is shown by the case of Germany. Although its level of economic growth was good, per capita energy consumption declined in Germany from 1980 to the mid-1990s, largely because of the ecologically sophisticated policies adopted there.

Globalization and the regulation of corporate power

The regulation of corporate power, of course, is closely connected to problems of ecological management. Some of the world's biggest companies are now in the area of biotechnology. Industrial corporations are also often prime sources of environmental pollution, as well as other policies that might ride roughshod over ecological considerations. In tackling these and other issues of corporate responsibility, modernizing democrats wherever possible should seek to work with business rather than against it. Business groups and organizations should be actively enlisted to help create a society, on a local as well as a world level, in which they play a responsible part.

Yet left-of-centre governments mustn't shirk confronting corporate interests where it is necessary to do so – and it often *is* necessary to do so. Corporations don't, as the title of one well-known book puts it, 'rule the world',[14] but we should actively resist any and every development that might cause such an assertion to come true.

Government should seek to:

(1) Enforce competition policies nationally and internationally. Sometimes the global economy is offered as a rationale for why regulations on monopoly should be relaxed – on the grounds that very large corporations have to compete with others of comparable size in the world marketplace. But the net effect is to project monopoly onto a global scale. A study in the mid-1990s looked at the concentration ratios of twelve global industries, investigating the proportion of world markets controlled by the leading five corporations. The highest ratio is in consumer durables, where 70% of the world market is in the hands of the top five companies. The top five control more than 50% in the car, airline, electronic components and steel industries. They have more than 40% of sales in the oil, personal computer and media industries.

The implementation of national policies can have a direct effect on monopolies in transnational markets, since the large corporations have their home bases in a limited number of nations – above all, in the US. Enforceable international legislation and controls are, of course, also required. An important test case is looming at the moment. In November 1999, Microsoft was found poten-

---

[14] David Korten, *When Corporations Rule the World*. West Hartford, CT: Kumarian Press, 1995.

tially to have contravened the US antitrust laws. The initial judgement against the company concluded that it had monopoly control over personal computer operating systems, and that it used that control in ways detrimental to consumers. The full legal conclusions have not yet been issued, but they could entail the break-up of the company. Microsoft currently owns 90% of the market in personal computer operating systems software. One possibility is that the corporation will be carved up into separate companies; another is that it will be obliged to share its Windows source code with its competitors.

Legal procedures progress slowly, especially as compared to the flux of the high-tech industries. Microsoft has put through a series of deals with telecommunication companies and is moving into other areas as well. The target of the antitrust legislators is thus a shifting one, and at the time of writing it is far from clear what the eventual outcome will be.

(2) Collaborate with third-sector groups and non-governmental organizations in monitoring corporate activities, on a world-wide basis as well as in more limited contexts. Business corporations aren't the only actors to have set up global networks. Many other groups have done so too. They form a countervailing power to the multinational companies, and such power is not so unbalanced in favour of the corporations as might be assumed at first sight. In the global age, it is no longer possible for companies to hide away what they do in one part of the world from the gaze of interested groups and associations.

Consumer groups, moreover, have the capacity to hit corporations where it hurts, by directly affecting company profits. The Brent Spar episode in 1995 marked something of a turning-point in this respect. The Shell oil company discovered that ecological groups, especially when combined with consumer sanctions, could have a great impact on their business. Shell and other large oil-producing firms have since reversed their position on ecological concerns. They have come to see the management of ecological risk and the promotion of environmental sustainability as issues to which they should make a positive contribution.

The recent history of Monsanto, one of the world's biggest biotechnology companies, is also instructive in this respect. Monsanto invested very large sums in the production of genetically modified crops and initially had great success in the American market. Robert Shapiro, the head of Monsanto, proclaimed that the promotion of these crops in the US was the most 'successful launch of any technology ever, including the plough'.[15]

The reactions of ecological groups across the world, however, and of many among the general public, have severely dented Monsanto's ambitions. Hostility was particularly marked in Europe. In the first six months of 1999 US corn exports to Europe dropped by over 90%. American farmers are starting to revert to traditional seeds rather than continue with the GM ones. In the same year, the US agriculture secretary Dan Glickman began an in-

[15] John Vidal, 'How Monsanto's mind was changed.' *Guardian* (9 October 1999).

vestigation into whether the links between his department and companies like Monsanto were too close.

Learning of this investigation, Deutsche Bank, the largest bank in Europe, recommended that institutional investors sell Monsanto shares. Shares in the company lost 35% of their value, at a time when the average value of shares on Wall Street went up by 30%. Mr Shapiro subsequently said: 'We forgot to listen. We have irritated and antagonised more people than we have persuaded . . . our confidence in biotechnology has been widely seen as arrogance and condescension.' He promised a much broader and more open dialogue than the company had considered necessary hitherto. Subsequently, however, the company came under great pressure from analysts and investment advisers to break itself up. Many investors became convinced that the social protest its policies had provoked had so severely damaged its economic prospects that its continuation as an integrated company was impossible. While its drugs business was still highly valued on the stock market, by October 1999 the value of its agricultural chemicals business had declined dramatically.

(3)   Foster corporate responsibility through a mixture of active encouragement, including tax incentives, and the rigorous policing of corporate behaviour. Rogue corporations exist, as do rogue nations, and both are going to need special treatment on the part of national governments and international law. But there is no reason why responsible corporate conduct shouldn't be underpinned both nationally and internationally. 'Responsibility' is a

wide and potentially vague notion, and it is obvious that companies might pay it no more than token respect. On the other hand, some corporations have led the way in promoting responsible corporate behaviour. The Levi-Strauss clothing company, for example, sought to be an industry leader in this respect. Robert Haas, the chief executive, introduced standards of practice that were to be observed in all company plants across the globe.

(4)   Ensure that corporate responsibility gives full weight to ecological responsibility, in the various meanings which that term carries. This prescription has to include the corporate exploitation of poorer areas of the world. Toxic dumping has been carried on by corporations and to some extent by countries. For instance, much of the Japanese aluminium- and copper-processing industry has been re-located to poorer parts of South-East Asia. A Japanese-financed and -built copper-smelting plant in Leyte in the Philippines exists on 400 acres of land acquired very cheaply. The emissions from the plant contain large amounts of pollutants harmful to the local environment and human health. The company avoids the much stricter environmental regulations that exist in Japan.[16]

(5)   Act, and act determinedly where necessary, to keep the public spaces of civil society open, including a public sphere of communication. There are large areas of public life that should not be commercialized – although having an open public sphere means that where the boundaries should be drawn can be debated. Govern-

---

[16] Korten, *When Corporations Rule the World*, p. 223.

ment may often need to take the lead: parks, schoolrooms, waterways, common land and other areas should be protected from advertising and commercialization. Government should also initiate 'publicization' where necessary – the return of commercialized space to public use. For example, shopping malls or large superstores are best accepted with a limited rental life-span, such that in future these areas could be turned over to different use. Communities in countries as far apart as Korea, Brazil and the US have introduced such ideas.

Media regulation is an inescapable element of the control and development of public space. There is no area where anti-monopoly policy is more important. Since the media shape public opinion, and since in democratic countries politicians must listen to public opinion, for obvious reasons it is difficult for political leaders to resist monopoly media power.

But they must strive to do so, going with the grain of technological change rather than against it. Existing models of public broadcasting mostly involve fighting a rearguard action against change – for instance, keeping a number of channels as state-run and state-financed. It may be necessary for governments to dig in their heels on these issues, to hold back commercialization. But there is also freedom in diversity. The proliferation of media technologies now becoming available both poses a threat to existing forms of public services and at the same time offers new opportunities. Specialized education or public information services can be carried on digital TV; interactive media offer possibilities for public debates on issues of general interest.

(6) Encourage corporations to adopt employee share ownership schemes where feasible, and favour employee buy-outs of failing companies where adequate capital can be generated. In most countries, stock option plans are available far more often to directors and managers than to other employees. Yet in the US 9 million employees are covered by such plans, in some 10,000 companies. Tax incentives could provide the motivation for more companies to join in. Tax breaks could be given to firms that maintain a certain level of employee ownership. Preferential access to loans could be made available to firms embracing ownership schemes, or to employees acquiring shares.

There is reason to think that employee ownership plans might become more common with the development of knowledge-intensive industries. Network restructuring in larger enterprises, the decline of bureaucracy and the emergence of many new smaller firms are all relevant trends. Deferred profit-sharing had been introduced in 15% of firms with over 100 employees in the US by the early 1990s. High-tech industries seem to be in the vanguard. Equity is the most frequent form of non-wage benefit sought by workers in IT firms.

In the more corporatist economies of continental Europe employee participation has traditionally taken a different form. As these economies undergo change, however, there are possibilities of using share-option schemes as a means of democratizing the transition. In France, for example, privatization has created a network of powerful interlocking companies. If a more supportive tax and legal environment were developed, some shares could be purchased on behalf of the employees of these companies, perhaps held in pension plans.

(7)   Encourage corporations and unions to work together on economic restructuring in the face of technological change. Once more we need to look for new models here rather than relying on the old ones. There are situations in which management and unions are in a situation of interest conflict, and where unions need to protect the labour force from damaging corporate policies. Yet there are just as many other circumstances in which only active cooperation can offer such protection. Unions now exist in more pluralistic milieux than they used to, and should collaborate with other groups, such as third-sector associations, too.

As well as dealing directly with employees, unions now also need to promote employability and skills training. Unions could negotiate links for workers to the wider community, help provide access to lifelong learning and form private-sector purchasing cooperatives. 'If today's union leaders hope to stem the decline in their members' economic security, including the loss of traditional benefits, they've got to become much more creative about how those benefits might be organised, accessed and financed. With the emergence of a very new sort of workforce that is much more independent of the employment relationship, unionists must simply get smarter about how benefits could be provided with less dependence on employers.'[17]

[17] Jeff Gates, *The Ownership Solution*. London: Allen Lane, 1998, pp. 109–10.

Underlying many of these observations is a problem too complex to deal with at any length in a study such as this: in the global age, what form of capitalism should modernizing social democrats support? 'Shareholder capitalism', as practised in the US and UK, is quite often contrasted with 'stakeholder capitalism', more characteristic of the central and northern European economies and Japan. The comparison may be a crude one, but it isn't without value. Shareholder capitalism is capitalism in its stripped-down version, with management concerned, in principle, with maximizing returns to its owners. In the stakeholder model, a wider range of individuals, groups and communities is recognized to have a stake in the fortunes of the corporation. The Rhineland type of shareholder system integrates corporatist coordination with worker participation on management committees.

The view of the future of capitalism held by the neoliberal right is simple. Shareholder capitalism – the Anglo-Saxon version of capitalism – is destined to sweep all before it, not only in Europe, but elsewhere in the world too. It is far more fluid, responsive and adaptable to change than the stakeholder model. Some on the more traditional left, on the other hand, have turned their attention to a defence of stakeholder capitalism. Once critical of corporatist capitalism, seen as merely a token recognition of workers' rights, they have come to regard it as the best way of smoothing over the rough edges of the market system. If the state can no longer aspire to take over the commanding heights of the economy, in stakeholder capitalism state institutions, in conjunction with business and unions, can continue to play a significant role.

151

Neither of these positions is especially persuasive. The idea that there is one form of capitalism towards which others will, or should, move on a global level doesn't make much sense. A variety of different forms, varying according to culture, history and type of economy, will surely continue to coexist. Stakeholder capitalism, in its various guises in Europe and elsewhere, has too many achievements to its name to be easily relinquished, and is too closely integrated with other social institutions to be altered in the short term. From the other side, the Anglo-Saxon economies are not about to move far towards the stakeholder model.

It must be time to stop thinking of overall models to which any particular country should aspire. Instead, some of the principles of corporate responsibility just listed can be developed, or fought for, within varying national and transnational contexts. It is quite possible that neither shareholder nor stakeholder capitalism can survive intact in a longer time-frame. The more aggressive forms of shareholder capitalism risk destroying the social and civic frameworks that make a capitalist economy viable in the first place. This is the core objection of third way politics to the market fundamentalism of the neoliberals. Yet along with its virtues, stakeholder capitalism tends to bring major limitations and flaws. It isn't quick enough on its feet to respond to the world in which we find ourselves. More than that, rather than being democratic, seen by the standards of an open information society it is often closed and clientelist. Decisions are taken by interlocking elites, worker involvement is nominal, banking loans are arranged through personal contacts, cartels are the norm rather than the exception. The two systems – or rather the diversity of forms they contain – will continue to coexist. But policies promoting responsible capitalism relevant to both need to be pioneered.

Old wars and new wars

The 'downward pressure' for local autonomy produced by globalization has greatly altered the composition of states on an international level. In 1983 there were 144 recognized nations in the world. By the late 1990s this number had grown to just under 200. More will certainly come into being over the next few years, as local ethnic groups and 'nations without a state' press for greater autonomy.[18] In such a situation, the nature of war is changing, although no one can possibly say whether or not this is happening in a permanent way. States may be multiplying, but territory is not as important to their power and prosperity as it once was, since natural resources count for less. The new sources of ideological conflict, such as those involving religious fundamentalism, for the most part stretch across, or affect specific regions within, nations. Most conflicts are likely to happen in local contexts, rather than being between nation states. Thus in 1997 twenty-five major armed struggles took place. Only one of these, between India and

[18] Montserrat Guibernau, *Nations Without States*. Cambridge: Polity Press, 1999.

153

Pakistan, was between states, and this remained quite confined; all the others were internal in character.

Mary Kaldor argues that the wars which happened in the 1980s and 1990s differ distinctively from 'old wars' between nations – and that they reflect the changes brought about by globalization.[19] The conflicts that have happened in ex-Yugoslavia, for example, are not a throwback to the history of the Balkans, but were much more of a contemporary phenomenon. The new wars are physically localized, but they typically involve a diversity of transnational agencies and relationships – international TV crews, foreign advisers, UN groups and non-governmental organizations.

These conflicts occur where state legitimacy has crumbled and there is criminality, corruption and a break-up of civil society. The aims of the warring parties are less concerned with geopolitical considerations than with aggressive forms of identity conflicts, often following ethnic lines. The beliefs, anxieties and hatreds that fuel identity struggles look back to ancient traditions, but they do not directly derive from them. Rather, traditional divisions, which may have remained latent or largely forgotten for many years, are resurrected and called into play as a means of focusing present-day discontents.

The warfare that occurs in such situations tends to avoid large-scale battles. The warring groups try to advance their aims via political control of the population, expelling or attacking those who are regarded as alien. In such wars there has been a marked increase in the

[19] Mary Kaldor, *New and Old Wars*. Cambridge: Polity Press, 1999.

numbers of refugees, since it is civilians who are targeted. A century ago, military casualties in war outstripped civilian casualties by a factor of 8:1. In current conflicts, this ratio is reversed. In nation-state wars, the war economy was centralized and hierarchical. The new war economies are decentralized and anarchic, with support for the fighting parties coming from outside governments, drugs, illegal trade in arms, or plunder. Such war economies exist, or have recently existed, in the Balkans, the Caucasus, and central and west Africa. Through all this stalks global mass culture. Militiamen wear brand-name sneakers and sport baseball caps. The Albanians in Kosovo received broadcasts in Albanian from Switzerland via their satellite dishes.

The longer-term consequences of the conflict in Kosovo, as well as in other parts of ex-Yugoslavia, remain to be determined. The 'new interventionism' has come in for a great deal of critical attack – from the right, where many believe that states should be left to resolve their own problems, and from the old left, who see such interventionism as a cloak for American or Western power politics. But taking globalization seriously means rejecting both of these positions. Globalization has redefined the sovereignty of states, while individual rights have become the subject of an expanding body of international law. The intervention in Kosovo, which was not legitimated by the UN, and that in East Timor, which was, raise difficult issues of principle and practice. Yet the results of inaction were displayed in a horrific manner by the mass murders in Rwanda. The interventions undertaken by the international community thus far have at most met with limited success. Some groups have been protected or otherwise cared for, and tenuous ceasefires agreed, but there is no case where the underlying problems that caused the conflicts have been effectively dealt with. International peace-keeping troops have normally been far too thin on the ground to be able to do more than stand by when major episodes of violence unfold, and have sometimes been humiliated.

As in the case of global economic disturbances, we need to find more satisfactory forms of crisis management – but the most important strategies have to concern preventing crises from occurring in the first place. Since the new wars differ from nation-state conflicts, we cannot apply traditional thinking to them. The aim of the parties involved in the new wars is political control through exclusion, and the tactics used are intimidation and terror. Hence it is extremely difficult to re-establish a framework of political legitimacy and law. External agencies seeking to set up such a framework tend to be similarly powerless, for the same reasons. 'Infringement of sovereignty' has no real meaning in such circumstances, and is perhaps simply the wrong way to think about them. The new wars are both local and global, since there are a variety of external groups and organizations present on the scene. There is no such thing as non-intervention, because outside involvement is one of their defining features.

The policies that might help cope with the aftermath of the new wars are the same as those that would best prevent them happening in the first place. At the moment, the main approach is to attempt to achieve a negotiated solution between the warring groups – a notion based on traditional diplomacy. The problems are obvious. Negotiations may depend upon individuals who have been indicted as war criminals. Neither power-sharing agreements nor territorial partition provide workable solutions, while refugees are a source of continuing tension. Moreover, the warring groups have only a limited capability to enforce accords that are reached, because their power is founded upon anxiety and fear.

Pacification can only really happen if institution-building is incorporated into negotiations, drawing upon cosmopolitan principles established in international law. Spaces for the reconstruction of civil society need to be established or kept open. Kaldor gives a variety of examples. In Armenia and Azerbaijan, for instance, NGOs were able to negotiate with local authorities to set up a peace corridor, where hostages or prisoners of war were released and an effective dialogue between civil society and political agencies established. The conflict there was successfully defused. Dialogues between groups other than the warring parties themselves seem to be the key. There are actually far more cases where such processes have prevented, or put an end to, armed struggle than ones that have culminated in large-scale violence – showing that there is nothing utopian about this approach. Of course, these situations do not become a focus of world-wide attention in the way that open and protracted conflicts do.

Generalizing further from such examples, we can say that the focus should not be upon peacekeeping as ordinarily defined, but upon the enforcement of cosmopolitan principles. International military forces should accept, and attempt to implement, such principles, since otherwise they will simply become another party to the conflict. Impartiality is not the same as neutrality, although the two are often confused. Neutrality means taking no stand against whatever acts conflicting parties may engage in – the position of organizations such as the International Red Cross. Impartiality implies the enforcement of norms of international law where they are violated by either or both warring factions. An assertive reconstruction of an integrated civil order needs to be combined, where national and international resources allow, with dedicated programmes for replacing damaged infrastructure, housing and public services.

Realpolitik is not going to disappear from the global system in the near future, nor should it. We are far from a world in which codes of humanitarian law can be applied by international agencies regardless of who breaks them. China was accepted back into the international community shortly after the events in Tiananmen Square, and in spite of its persistent human rights abuses in Tibet. Arguably this was entirely the right course of action, since turning such a country into a pariah state could provoke international tensions leading to major war. Yet in the global era states, like transnational corporations, cannot escape the surveillance of the wider global community. As the number of democratic countries in the world grows, local groups subject to discrimination or oppression have access to international audiences to whom to air their grievances. We can make progress towards a world in which even the largest states conform to emerging codes of international law.

Global democracy

Even allowing for the increase in the number of states, a higher proportion of countries today are democratic than thirty years ago. Some argue that most of the newly democratic societies are only superficially changed – they are still run by self-interested oligarchies. Thus, in Africa, countries that have formally become democracies are often highly corrupt and elections are rigged. Fledgling democracies in Latin America are fighting to survive in the face of social disorder in both the cities and the countryside. In the Middle East, most countries are openly non-democratic while, with the exception of India, Asian democracy is at best poorly developed.

It would be wrong, however, to take too gloomy a view of global democratization. Detailed comparisons across countries show conclusively that the progression of democracy is real. There are good reasons to suppose that intensifying globalization actively promotes democracy, even in nations that may have little history of it. Globalization is driven in some large part by new systems of communication which, together with changes in everyday life, alter citizens' relation to the state. Authoritarian political power is not only much harder to sustain than in the past, it is more easily punctured and dissolved.

The further development of democracy within states could be greatly enhanced by the construction of transnational forms of democracy. Taking globalization seriously means emphasizing that democratization cannot be confined to the level of the nation state. To seek to

159

build democratic institutions above the level of the nation is again not a utopian aim. Such a process is already in the course of development, in the shape of the European Union. The EU began life essentially as a Cold War project, but it has to be seen today as a pioneering response to globalization. There is a basic difference between the EU and international organizations such as the United Nations. The UN is composed of representatives of sovereign nations. By contrast in the EU, for the first time in history, individual nations have voluntarily given up aspects of their sovereignty, substantive and legal, in order to pool their common resources.

The EU is not a super nation state, nor is there any likelihood that it might or could become one. It isn't a form of federalism either. It is difficult to categorize in traditional political terms precisely because it is a novel experiment, an attempt to develop governmental structures different from those that have existed before. As such, it confronts numerous difficulties. It might sound odd to offer the EU as an example – the prime example – of democratization above the level of the nation, since it is so often criticized for its 'democratic deficits'. The union has been largely constructed by political elites; the European Commission is heavily bureaucratic; the European Parliament lacks much influence; and in most EU countries voters take little interest in the European elections.

Yet the EU was certainly not constructed against the wishes of the majority of citizens in its member states. Moreover, a range of short- and longer-term measures can be introduced that would produce greater democracy as well as more popular legitimacy. Some of the prescriptions for democratizing democracy within nations also apply directly to the EU. Greater transparency, rooting out corruption, loosening bureaucratic hierarchies, devolving some of the power now held in Brussels, having direct elections for a range of major positions – these and other innovations are feasible and necessary.

The most problematic issues concern the authority of the European Parliament. Undoubtedly there should be a shift in power towards it and away from the Commission. But other possibilities need to be considered, including the forming of genuinely European parties. It isn't fanciful to suppose that similar organizations to the EU will emerge in other parts of the world, where at the moment there are only trading blocs. Proposals to that effect have been made, and widely discussed, in the Americas and in Asia. Such developments could potentially serve as a platform for a global form of cosmopolitan democracy.

Rather than treating the EU as distinctively European – that is, as specific to a particular geographical area – we might regard it as a bridgehead to a more globalizing transnational democratic system. Various possibilities lie open to be explored. The EU itself, particularly through its courts, could play a role in helping to promote a global cosmopolitan regime. Rules and standards of international behaviour, concerning in particular human rights and humanitarian law, need to be generalized. The EU could take the lead in tying trade contracts and financial assistance to substantive acceptance of such transnational codes. More ambitiously, if analogues to the EU come into being elsewhere, they could be the basis of regional parliaments, on the model of the European Parliament, and could send delegates to a remodelled world assembly.[20]

Some observers see the post-1989 world as likely to become ever more anarchic. The controlling influence of the Cold War has disappeared, unleashing a host of conflicting forces – leading to the splintering of nation states, the breakdown of civil order, and multiple episodes of violence.[21] It is true that on each of the major dimensions of globalization crisis is never far away. Moreover, in a world of increasingly interdependent systems, when things go wrong, they can go very wrong. If the world financial system were to go into meltdown, the consequences could be greater than the Great Crash of 1929. Were global warming to proceed unchecked, there could be turmoil in the world's climate. If global economic divisions become larger and larger, the result could be violent clashes between the privileged and the disinherited.

Yet the very existence of these and other cataclysmic possibilities should make us redouble our efforts to construct more effective global regulatory institutions. Without them, the coming century could prove even more brutal and devastating than that which has just closed.

---

[20] David Held, *Democracy and Global Order*. Cambridge: Polity Press, 1995.
[21] Robert D. Kaplan, *The Ends of the Earth*. London: Macmillan, 1997.

Conclusion

In conclusion, I should emphasize again that it doesn't matter whether or not the term 'third way' is used to refer to the ideas discussed in this book. What is at issue is making left of centre values count in a world undergoing profound change. It might be helpful to go back over some of the main themes and arguments. Third way politics, as I conceive of it, is not an attempt to occupy a middle ground between top-down socialism and free-market philosophy. It is concerned with restructuring social democratic doctrines to respond to the twin revolutions of globalization and the knowledge economy.

Each of these refers to a complex array of transformations, and there can be no question of saying that either is simply 'good' or 'bad'. Both, however, offer many potential benefits, and social democrats should take a positive rather than a defensive attitude towards them. Third way politics is not, as it is so often portrayed, a capitulation to neoliberalism. On the contrary, it emphasizes the core importance of active government and the public sphere. The public sphere does not coincide with the domain of the state. State institutions can diminish or discredit the realm of the public when they become oversized, bureaucratic or otherwise unresponsive to citizens' needs. The neoliberals were right to criticize the state in these respects, but wrong to suppose that the public good can be better supplied by markets.

Loss of state capacity over the past two or three decades has not been brought about only by globalization. It has come also from the endogenous crisis of the state. The restructuring of state and government can restore that capacity. The state continues to have a fundamental role to play in economic life as in other areas. It cannot replace either markets or civil society, but needs to intervene in each. Government should seek to create macroeconomic stability, promote investment in education and infrastructure, contain inequality and guarantee opportunities for individual self-realization. A strong welfare system, not a minimal safety net, is a core part of this package.

The citizen is not the same as the consumer, and freedom is not to be equated with the freedom to buy and sell in the marketplace. Markets do not create or sustain ethical values, which have to be legitimized through democratic dialogue and sustained through public action. On the other hand the left needs to drop the idea that markets are a necessary evil. There is no known alternative to the market economy any longer; market competition generates gains that no other system can match. The chance of economic prosperity is only one of these. Markets do not create citizenship, but they can contribute to it and even to the reduction of inequality.

A market economy can only function effectively within a framework of social institutions and if grounded in a developed civil society – a proposition that holds on a global level as well as more locally. The good society is one that strikes a balance between government, markets and the civil order. The protection and enhancement of the civil sphere is a key preoccupation of third way politics. It is a mistake just to counterpose the state to markets. Without a stable civil society, incorporating norms of trust and social decency, markets cannot flourish and democracy can be undermined.

We need to reconnect these three spheres by means of a new social contract, appropriate to an age where globalization and individualism go hand in hand. The new contract stresses both the rights and responsibilities of citizens. People should not only take from the wider community, but give back to it too. The precept 'no rights without responsibilities' applies to all individuals and groups. Government must maintain a regulatory role in many contexts, but as far as possible it should become a facilitator, providing resources for citizens to assume responsibility for the consequences of what they do.

A further tenet of third way politics – wherever possible invest in human capital – is closely bound up with this perspective. It is a guiding theme of welfare reform, as well as of the actions government must take to react to the knowledge economy. An active supply-side policy, placing a premium upon education, is essential. The aim is to create a high-employment economy – recognizing that nowadays many people have to reconcile work with domestic obligations. This approach does not imply a downgrading of the needs of those outside the labour market. They should be 'invested in' just as much as others. Positive welfare means attacking problems of dependency, isolation and lack of self-fulfilment wherever they arise.

A basic part of the third way project is responding seriously to public concerns about crime and the decay of family life. Social democrats should not be afraid to be tough where previously they have been tender. Crime is a major problem in most contemporary societies and should be treated as such. Many forms of criminality are closely bound up with inequality and deprivation. Yet it is by now well established that increasing prosperity, even when it is widely shared, is not automatically accompanied by an overall decline in crime. Moreover, coping with crime is an immediate issue for those directly affected by it.

It is often thought, even by some of the modernizers, that adopting a third way position means diluting a concern with inequality. It seems as though the modernizers are deserting the values of the left while the traditionalists are preserving them, or would do so if their policies were implemented. After all, the more traditional left wants existing welfare systems to stay intact, and to keep taxes and levels of welfare spending high, even if this implies large state deficits.

But this view is false. We cannot tackle inequalities by further extending such policies, which have reached their limits. A different approach is needed. Sound fiscal and macroeconomic policies can reduce poverty and social exclusion as well as reverse trends towards increasing economic inequality more generally. It used to be assumed that if deficit spending was reduced, public investment would have to decline, while poorer groups would be most adversely affected. Neither of these assumptions turns out to be valid. Combined with appropriate macro-economic measures, deficit reduction can foster high labour market participation and economic expansion. In tandem with active social investment, this can in turn lead to the involvement of groups previously marginal to the labour market.

In this book, as in my earlier one, I have concentrated on the industrial countries. The debate between the old and new left in fact ranges much more widely. The third way has been the subject of intense controversy in many countries in Asia and in Central and South America. As Luiz Bresser Pereira points out, the debate in the South has followed similar lines to that in the more developed parts of the world. In the developing as well as developed world, 'for the new right globalization is an opportunity; for the old left, a threat; for the new left, a challenge'.[1]

In the South and elsewhere, this challenge must be met by rebuilding state capacity, in conjunction with international regulation. The modernizing left recognizes that the interests of the developed and developing countries are often the same, rather than always contradictory. It

---

[1] Luiz Carlos Bresser Pereira, 'The New Left viewed from the South.' Text presented at Third Way Seminar, Industrial Federation of Rio de Janeiro (11 November 1998): 13.

does not make the mistake of supposing that the problems of the poorer countries come mainly from external factors. The large-scale abolition of debt will be a welcome spur to development, but in the longer term debt should be countered by generating trade surpluses, rather than by a free and easy attitude to borrowing. Gaining the confidence of financial markets is crucial, and depends upon internal reforms in which the state must take the lead.

Finally, let me say my aim in responding to critiques of the third way from the traditional left is not to widen the rifts that already exist. I hope in fact that my analysis will contribute to healing them, or at a minimum promote a helpful dialogue. All too often in the past squabbles on the left have undermined its influence, and none of us should want the same to happen again.

Third Way Bibliography

Blair, Tony. *The Third Way*. London: Fabian Society, 1998.
Sets out an 'official' approach to third way politics. Argues that we must leave behind 'statist' approaches as well as breaking decisively with free-market philosophies. The pamphlet was widely disseminated and has been discussed in a variety of different countries.

Blair, Tony, and Gerhard Schröder. *Europe: The Third Way – die Neue Mitte*. London: Labour Party and SPD, 1999.
A statement of third way principles endorsed by two of Europe's major political leaders. Largely ignored in the UK, the Blair–Schröder paper stimulated a great deal of controversy in Germany.

Blundell, John, and Brian Gosschalk. *Beyond Left and Right*. London: Institute of Economic Affairs, 1997.
An interesting analysis of changing voting attitudes, showing that the categories of left and right have less relevance in categorizing people's political beliefs than once they had.

Bobbio, Norberto. *Left and Right*. Cambridge: Polity Press, 1996.
Argues that the realignment of the left doesn't make the dis-

169

tinction of left and right obsolete. Rather, it still marks a fundamental value difference. The left seeks to achieve a more or less egalitarian society whereas the right considers inequality to be inevitable.

Collins, Philip. 'A game of give and take.' In *The Third Way*, ed. Social Market Foundation, 12–16. London: Social Market Foundation, 1999.

Claims that the relationship of business and New Labour is problematic: the government's insistence on social responsibility collides with shareholder interests and its emphasis on domestic competition endangers firms' preparations for world markets.

Crick, Bernard. 'Still missing: a public philosophy?' *Political Quarterly* 68/4 (1997): 344–51.

A reflection on the tasks facing the British Labour Party following the 1997 election. The author argues that a 'clear public philosophy' needs to be developed, different from the ideas of the old left.

Crouch, Colin. 'The terms of the neo-liberal consensus.' *Political Quarterly* 68/4 (1997): 352–60.

An analysis of the reasons for the enduring qualities of social democracy, together with a discussion of comparative developments across Europe.

Cuperus, René, and Johannes Kandel, eds. *Transformation in Progress: European Social Democracy*. Amsterdam: Friedrich-Ebert-Stiftung, 1998.

Various academics and politicians discuss the challenges facing centre-left parties across Europe. The issues include the democratization of European institutions and the impact of globalization on welfare regimes and inequality.

Dahrendorf, Ralf. 'Whatever happened to liberty?' *New Statesman* (6 September 1999): 25–7.

The author discerns an 'authoritarian streak' in third way

politics. The emphasis on referenda and focus groups as well as the thrust of welfare to work betray a neglect of classic liberal values.

Democratic Leadership Council–Progressive Policy Institute. *The New Progressive Declaration: A Political Philosophy for the Information Age.* Washington, DC: DLC–PPI, 1996.

Argues that a new progressive politics is needed to respond to the twin demands of globalization and the coming of the information age. We are living through a period of change as profound as that which initiated the 'old progressivism' seventy-five years ago.

Esping-Andersen, Gøsta. 'Positive-sum solutions in a world of trade-offs?' In *Welfare States in Transition: National Adaptations in Global Economics,* ed. Gøsta Esping-Andersen, 256–67. London: Sage, 1996.

The political coalitions in most parts of Europe seem to favour the status quo of the welfare state. This is problematic since reform is needed in order to achieve an alternative egalitarian model in a post-industrial world.

Etherington, David. 'From welfare to work in Denmark: an alternative to free market policies?' *Policy & Politics* 26/2 (1998): 147–61.

Welfare reforms implemented in Denmark in 1994 demonstrate that partnerships between local government and trade unions are crucial for successful welfare-to-work schemes. The UK approach appears to be too free-market-oriented to appreciate this fact.

Faux, Jeff. 'Lost on the third way.' *Dissent* 46/2 (Spring 1999): 67–76.

A highly critical discussion of third way politics, concentrating upon the American Democratic Party. Faux argues that the third way is simply unable to confront the realities of the global era, and in particular ignores problems pro-

171

duced by inequalities of wealth and power.

Finlayson, Alan. 'Third way theory.' *Political Quarterly* 70/3 (1999): 271–9.

Places current third way theory in the context of the political debates of the 'New Left' of the 1980s. Although third way thinkers and analysts of 'New Times' share a lot in their respective diagnoses of society, their political agendas differ.

Fountain, Jane E. 'Social capital: a key enabler of innovation.' In *Investing in Innovation*, ed. L. M. Branscomb and J. H. Keller, 85–111. Cambridge, MA: MIT Press, 1998.

The author describes how inter-organizational linkages have improved economic performance and innovative capacity in US firms. Government policies should thus seek to foster such alliances.

Galston, William A., and Elaine C. Kamarck. 'Five realities that will shape 21st-century politics.' *Blueprint: Ideas for a New Century* 1 (Fall 1998): 7–22.

The political agenda has to be adjusted to the new political realities of the knowledge economy, which has created workers with different concerns and interests from the past.

Gamble, Andrew, and Tony Wright. *The New Social Democracy* (special issue of *Political Quarterly*, vol. 70). Oxford: Blackwell, 1999.

A collection of articles discussing the resurgence of the centre-left in Europe. The contributors discuss the reforms social democrats need to make to respond to social and economic change. The editors argue that the third way has to be 'a new social democracy for our times'.

Giddens, Anthony. *The Third Way: The Renewal of Social Democracy*. Cambridge: Polity Press, 1998.

This book argues that developing a third way is a necessity in modern politics. The problems facing the world today require a new, robust and wide-ranging social-democratic agenda.

Gilbert, Neil. 'Remodeling social welfare.' *Society* 35/5 (1998): 8–13.

Explains the way in which recent reforms of the US welfare system contribute to the creation of an 'enabling welfare state'.

Glennerster, H. 'Which welfare states are most likely to survive?' *International Journal of Social Welfare* 8/1 (1999): 2–13.

Welfare states have to adapt to fundamental changes in society. Sustainable solutions will have to find a balance of labour market policy, fiscal strategy and the respective welfare regimes.

'Goldilocks politics.' *The Economist* (19 December 1998).

A critical discussion of third way politics from a market liberal position. Argues that the third way is an uncomfortable mix of rightist politics and left rhetoric.

Hall, Stuart. 'The great moving nowhere show.' *Marxism Today* (November/December 1998): 9–14.

A critical discussion of the aspirations of New Labour in the UK. According to Hall, the new directions taken by the British Labour Party in the end lead nowhere. Many of the core problems that a left-of-centre government should face up to are simply ignored. New Labour tries to please everyone; hence its policies lack edge or distinctiveness.

Halpern, David, and David Mikosz. *The Third Way*. London: Nexus, 1998.

This book summarizes a discussion on third way politics organized by Nexus, a UK think-tank. Given the diversity of perspectives, the authors conclude that the principles of the third way approach need to be stated with greater clarity.

173

Hargreaves, Ian, and Ian Christie, eds. *Tomorrow's Politics: The Third Way and Beyond*. London: Demos, 1998.
An edited collection discussing new political programmes for the centre-left in a variety of different areas.

Harrington, Pat. *The Third Way*. London: The Third Way Movement, 1998.
A response to the current debate about third way politics on the part of the Third Way Party, founded in 1990. The third way is described as a 'radical alternative to the establishment parties who have presided over decades of decline' in the UK.

Hombach, Bodo. *A New Awakening: The Politics of the New Centre in Germany*. Cambridge: Polity Press, 2000 (translation of *Aufbruch. Die Politik der Neuen Mitte*. Munich: Econ, 1998).
An analysis of the development of third way politics in Germany, using the description 'the new middle'. Hombach argues that the Social Democratic Party (SPD) needs to modernize in order to govern effectively, then govern in order to modernize. The book contains extensive proposals for the transformation of German politics. How far these will actually be realized is a matter of great controversy.

Kapstein, Ethan B. 'A global Third Way: social justice and the world economy.' *World Policy Journal* 15/4 (1998): 23–34.
To achieve the objectives of third way politics an international strategy is needed. The mobility of capital requires multilateral cooperation in taxation. The aim should be to join business to a broader social purpose.

Kapstein, Ethan B. *Sharing the Wealth: Workers and the World Economy*. New York and London: W. W. Norton, 1999.
Argues that the global economy requires international collaboration to secure social safety nets. Politicians have to achieve arrangements like the postwar Bretton Woods system

in order to secure labour standards and equal opportunity.

Kusnet, David, and Ruy Teixeira. 'The third way and the future of social democracy.' *Dissent* 46/3 (Summer 1999): 58–63.

The authors criticize a lack of clarity in the political-economic models of the centre-left parties in North America and western Europe. If they are to retain power as both popular and progressive forces they must devise more precise political strategies to ensure economic security for the twenty-first century.

Latham, Mark. 'Economic policy and the third way.' *Australian Economic Review* 31/4 (1998): 384–98.

The third way project must take economic policy seriously because a strong economy and a strong society go hand in hand. In contrast to the neoliberal emphasis on market freedoms, the third way sets its sights on education, entrepreneurialism and rewards for effort.

Latham, Mark. *Civilising Global Capital: New Thinking for Australian Labor.* St Leonards, NSW: Allen & Unwin, 1998.

The author suggests that it is possible to achieve economic prosperity whilst maintaining social standards in the age of mobile capital. Latham argues for an emphasis on education and research along with new fiscal strategies.

Leadbeater, Charles. *Living on Thin Air: The New Economy.* London: Viking, 1999.

A discussion of the knowledge economy, written by an author influential in the development of third way politics. Argues that social democrats must be prepared to be much more innovative than they have been so far if social democracy is to respond effectively to the new economic order.

Lukes, Steven. 'More than words?' In *The Third Way*, ed. Social Market Foundation, 17–20. London: Social Market

Foundation, 1999.

Claims that third way rhetoric seeks to conceal three basic political dilemmas: the question of taking equality seriously, the problem of community versus liberty, and the conflict between elitism and democracy.

Marquand, David. 'A philosophy that would not die.' *New Statesman* (26 February 1999).

Marquand attributes the resurgence of social democracy in Europe to the public demand for reining in the forces of neoliberal globalization. Compared with the mechanistic thinking of neoliberal and Marxian ideologies, social democracy still has a great deal to offer.

Merkel, Wolfgang. *The Third Ways of European Social Democracy at the End of the Twentieth Century*. Institut für Politische Wissenschaft, University of Heidelberg: Heidelberg, 1999.

An interesting and comprehensive discussion of the different 'third ways' taken by left-of-centre governments in the leading European countries. Contrasts political development in the UK, France, the Netherlands, Sweden and Germany.

Mouffe, Chantal. 'The radical centre: politics without an adversary.' *Soundings* 9 (1998): 11–23.

The author claims that the radicalism of New Labour is both misconceived and empty. The idea of a 'radical centre' has little sense to it. We need to insist on the distinction between left and right as well as decide who the true enemies of the left are.

Navarro, Vicenç. 'La tercera via: un análisis critico.' *Claves de Razón Práctica* 96 (October 1999).

Argues that the turn to third way politics on the part of various European left-of-centre parties is a basic mistake. The third way is not a social-democratic path at all, but a restatement of Christian Democratic ideals and policies.

Philpot, Robert. 'Why Bill Clinton is a hero.' *New Statesman* (19 July 1999): 21–2.

Argues that Bill Clinton's achievements have been radically underestimated by most people on the centre-left in Europe. Clinton's policies have not only created a strong economy but have also had positive results for social security and for diminishing economic inequality in the US.

Plender, John. 'A new third way.' *Prospect* (February 1998).

The author is looking for a third way of socially cohesive capitalism. As more and more job changes make it difficult to let employees share in prosperity through the workplace, he suggests the promotion of equity ownership as a viable option.

Pollard, Stephen. 'The only way is up.' In *The Third Way*, ed. Social Market Foundation, 3–6. London: Social Market Foundation, 1999.

In order to achieve equality New Labour must continue the project of breaking down the barriers to social mobility.

Roemer, John E. 'Egalitarian strategies.' *Dissent* 46/3 (Summer 1999): 64–74.

Argues that the left can rely on four strategies in order to achieve an egalitarian society: profit equalization, tax and transfer, education, and solidaristic wages. In terms of feasibility and payoff, education is the most promising strategy, but the others should not be dismissed.

Ruistin, Mike. 'A Third Way with teeth.' *Soundings* 11 (1999): 7–21.

Argues that the third way lacks substance but can in principle be developed to have more continuity with the basic ideals and policies of the left.

Ryan, Alan. 'Britain: recycling the third way.' *Dissent* 46/2 (Spring 1999): 77–80.

The author argues that the third way is a rehash of ideas

produced by the New Liberals many years ago – and an inferior version at that.

Sassoon, Donald. *The New European Left*. London: Fabian Society, 1999.

A discussion of the various views of the modernizing left in Europe, concentrating on Germany, France, Sweden and the Netherlands.

Sevenhuijsen, Selma. *Caring in the Third Way*. Leeds: Centre for Research on Family, Kinship and Childhood, University of Leeds, 1999.

Examines the possibilities of a third way approach to caring. As with other areas of social policy any reform must address the fundamental changes in contemporary society.

SPD–Grundwertekommission beim Parteivorstand. *Dritte Wege – Neue Mitte. Sozialdemokratische Markierungen für Reformpolitik im Zeitalter der Globalisierung*. Berlin: Parteivorstand der SPD, 1999.

This text by the 'basic value commission' of the German Social Democratic Party compares the different third way approaches of several European governments and formulates principles of a social-democratic reform agenda for the next century.

'The third way goes global.' *The New Democrat* 3 (May/June 1999).

Includes an account of the dialogue between Bill Clinton, Tony Blair, Gerhard Schröder, Massimo D'Alema and Wim Kok, held in Washington in 1998. Also contains several discussions of third way politics.

Torfing, Jacob. 'Workfare with welfare: recent reforms of the Danish welfare state.' *Journal of European Social Policy* 9/1 (1999): 5–28.

An interesting discussion of the introduction of welfare-to-work policies in Denmark. The author argues that these reforms have proved successful and have come to be an essential part of the Danish 'negotiated economy'.

Tuomioja, Erkki. 'Blairism may not work elsewhere in Europe.' Newsletter of the Finnish Institute in London (July 1998). Questions whether the policies developed by the British Labour Party have any relevance to more advanced Continental welfare states. Labour's reforms might mean a good deal in the context of the UK but are either familiar or irrelevant elsewhere.

Watrin, Christian. Europe's 'New' Third Way. Heritage Lectures 634 (7 May 1999), Heritage Foundation, Washington, DC, 1999. The author sees third way politics as a mere continuation of old social-democratic principles. He criticizes both approaches for basically advocating a paternalistic view of society, thus endangering individual freedom.

Westergaard, John. 'Where does the third way lead?' New Political Economy 4 (November 1999). A balanced discussion of third way issues, which includes an analysis of the ideas of Oskar Lafontaine and Christa Müller.

White, Stuart. Interpreting the 'Third Way': Not One Route, But Many. Mimeo, 1998. Available from http://netnexus.org/library/papers/white2.htm. White defines the third way in terms of the core values of opportunity, civic responsibility and community. Within this framework there is still room for disagreement. This pluralism is both a weakness and a strength of third way thinking.

Wilkinson, Helen. 'The family way: navigating a third way in family policy.' In Tomorrow's Politics: The Third Way and Beyond, ed. Ian Hargreaves and Ian Christie, 112–25. London: Demos, 1998.

The centre-left is well advised to take family policy seriously. While the right has traditionally juxtaposed the rhetoric of family values and an advocacy of free-market liberalism, the centre-left is in a position to actually combine the two.

Willets, David. 'Been there, done that.' In *The Third Way*, ed. Social Market Foundation, 7–11. London: Social Market Foundation, 1999.

Willets argues that welfare-to-work schemes alone cannot solve the unemployment problem. Lowering the obstacles to taking on unemployed people is as important as improving skills.

Index

Index

Index

Index

Index

Index

Index

Index

Index